Magic Quilted
MANDALAS

Sheila Finklestein

krause publications

700 East State Street, Iola, WI 54990-0001
www.krause.com

Please call or write for our free catalog of publications. Our toll-free number to place an order or obtain a free catalog is 800-258-0929 or please use our regular business telephone 715-445-2214 for editorial comment and further information.

Some product names in this book are registered trademarks of their respective companies:

The Original True Angle®
9° Circle Wedge Ruler®
15-degree Wedge Ruler®

Photography by Kris Kandler
Illustrations by Eric Merrill
Book design by Jan Wojtech
Manufactured in the United States of America

Library of Congress Cataloging-In-Publication Data

Finklestein, Sheila
Magic quilted mandalas
1. title   2. quilting   3. quilt design

ISBN 0-87341-635-X
CIP 98-87363

$\mathcal{A}$CKNOWLEDGMENTS

A project like a book is always a team effort, requiring many hands, much time, talent, and encouragement to complete. These are but a few of those special people who made "Mandalas" a reality:

My husband of more than 20 years who fully supports me in my creative spirit and countless projects. The kids, who realized early in life that Mom is "surgically attached" to her sewing machine. My mom, who still helps me find open spots in my life to indulge my creative compulsions. Debby Lee, who expertly created quilting designs and then quilted many of my quilts. Aunt Lori's patchwork pillows and Sandy Hemminger's hectic schedule that pushed me into quilting and landed the 9-degree wedge in my lap. My students who applauded the mandala class and wanted MORE. The patience and cheerleading of the Kindred Spirits and the Cascade Quilt Guilds: Peg who prodded me to start, Cindy and Debby who encouraged and kept me sane, and especially my mentor Cheryl Paul, who pruned, plugged, and prodded through my thoughts. You make it look like I really CAN walk and chew bubble gum!

And thanks to the following skillful, energetic professionals at Krause Publications: editor Amy Tincher-Durik, designer Jan Wojtech, and photographer Kris Kandler.

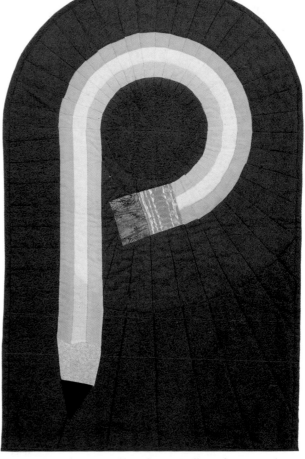

Persistence. This "pencil" quilt is a Bullseye layout with spacer strips. Pieced and quilted by Cheryl Paul.

PREFACE

MY MEDICINE WHEEL

I came to mandala-making after a major life crisis. At 34 years old I was diagnosed with breast cancer. Within the course of my treatment and healing, I discovered much about myself and my circle of life. I learned of Bernie Siegel's premise (in the book *Love, Medicine, and Miracles*) that in order to survive this or any crisis you must find what is important to you, your center, and dive in with both feet! For me that center was creativity—a process I had always expressed through sewing and, later, through quilting. I learned meditation and became aware of alternate theories of faith and existence. My quilting passion snowballed into a job and teaching. My job exposed me to the exploding quilt industry and its gadgets. All the while, my studies lead me to an awareness of mandalas and medicine wheels. I knew creativity, through quilting, was my personal medicine wheel—that each quilt project was a meditative, growth experience. I realized that many could benefit from this surge of creative energy and that I had an opportunity to share both the mysticism and the method with the quilting community around me.

My sharing began as classroom exercises designed to explore the uses of the 9° Circle Wedge Ruler, a tool designed to take the math mystery out of circle medallions. This simple design tool created deceptively intricate circular medallions without expert drafting skills. The wedge ruler opened the boundless design possibilities of mandalas to all levels of quilters. Anyone could take the wedge ruler and striped fabric to create a mandala design uniquely his or her own.

This book evolved from classroom experiences, both the delights and the disasters, of my students and myself. It can be shared by anyone with basic machine sewing and rotary cutting skills. Anyone with basic skills or beyond will be able to take these techniques and create a unique mandala. I hope you can find the balance of creativity in your own mandala.

Sheila Finklestein

Medicine Wheel. Approx. 60" x 60". Orange/red/magenta on teal. Bullseye layout with vertical "resized" spokes. Its "sister" quilt is Sundance (see page 32). Designed and pieced by Sheila Finklestein. Quilted by Debby Lee.

TABLE OF CONTENTS

*I*NTRODUCTION

MYSTICISM OF THE MANDALA

"The mandala is an ancient structure that supports harmony and balance. We can use its principles within our life and in our relationship with nature... Nourished by beauty, we can recover balance and openness. Once we heal the human heart, we will be empowered to heal the planet."
Tarthang Tulku, *Mandala Gardens*

Seeking a spiritual center to human existence has been present in most cultures throughout history. In many cultures a circular symbol with a definite center, a mandala, has been representative of that eternal spiritual force—a life-giving force beyond primitive understanding, a force ever-present and sustaining as the sun to their crops or the moon and stars to the cycles of their time. Circle symbols began to represent something greater, larger than themselves, a vastness. As ritual and prayer developed, so did meditation as a method of heightening awareness of the Great Spirit. In some eastern cultures, mandalas evolved as a meditative tool for reaching toward the eternal. In others, mandalas recorded the passage of time. Several Native American cultures considered losing touch with your greater power, or god-force, the source of misfortune or illness. In those native cultures, mandalas known as "magic circles" or "medicine wheels" are attributed with power in their own right. These circles act as an amulet, a kind of divine lightning rod. Magic circles and

medicine wheels are thought to correct imbalances in life cycles, changing misfortune into luck or curing illness.

Mandalas are often shown as a circle within a square, representing the duality of nature and the spirit. They can be bisected to indicate compass directions or the primal forces in nature. Mandalas can be painted, carved in stone, etched in metal, or traced in sand. In western cultures, circle symbols, such as haloes, stars, crosses, circuits, and webs, are everywhere. Early in this century, noted psychologist Carl Jung explored mandala symbols as an expression of "the self." For Jung, the drawing or creating of a mandala is a method of personal development. I believe that we function best when firmly centered in

the belief of a higher power. Recognizing a spirit center in our lives, its benevolent influence rotating and surrounding us, is the heart of the mandala tradition.

Making a mandala is a method of achieving balance between the realms of mental, physical, and emotional part of our being. Historically a way of achieving wholeness and centeredness, today mandalas are again surfacing as decorative and spiritual symbols, their swirling, hypnotic, visual movement inviting us into and beyond their center, inspiring us to find a center or balance in our own lives, motivating us to explore, and to create our own mystical magic circles.

Wheel of Fortune. Approx. 60" x 60". Red/mustard/black on cranberry. Bullseye layout with wedge-angled borders as 3-D inserts; has a five-patch center. Designed and pieced by Sheila Finklestein. Quilted by Debby Lee.

Chapter *1*

WHAT IS A QUILTED MANDALA?

In this book we will explore magic quilted mandalas and everything you need to create one, including the fabrics and tools needed as well as a discussion of the terms, design options, outer edge variations, centers, and mounting and finishing techniques you will need to be familiar with.

Quilted mandalas are made of striped fabric and require two tools: a rotary cutter and a 9- or 15-degree wedge ruler. Each mandala is formed from wedge-shaped pieces cut from the quilter's choice of striped fabric. Each wedge is equal to 9 or 15 degrees of a 360-degree full circle. The position of the 9- or 15-degree wedge ruler across the stripes at the time of cutting determines which design layout will occur.

There are two basic design layouts. In one, the ruler is placed straight across the stripes. In the other, the wedge ruler is angled across the stripes. In addition, several mandala designs use a combination of several cutting positions in a single mandala.

When using a 9° Circle Wedge Ruler, it takes 40 wedges to form a circle. With a 15-degree wedge tool, it takes 24. These wedges, when machine-stitched to each other, form a circular doughnut shape with an open center. The "doughnut hole" can be plugged with several types of centers (i.e. whole cloth or pieced units). Centers can narrowly cover the doughnut hole or overlap and conceal portion of the doughnut. The outer edge of the doughnut can be smooth, spiked, or scalloped. The mandala is then appliquéd to a background, bordered, and quilted.

Portal. Approx. 40" x 50". Variegated blues on blue. Spokes layout with wedge-angled borders (top only); has a cheater center. Its "sister" quilt is Rocky Road (see page 96). Designed, pieced, and quilted by Sheila Finklestein.

Castle Keep. 85" square bed quilt. 60-degree Chevron center with 60-degree Sawtooth fans in the corners. Its "sister" quilt is Twisted Ribbon Fan (see page 111). Pieced and quilted by Cindy Scott, 1994.

Chapter *2*

CHOOSING FABRIC

WHY STRIPES?

Stripes are the raw material of the mandala. You can sew individual strips of fabric together, but a faster and easier way is to buy striped fabric. Many striped fabrics contain fascinating flowers or motifs that add texture and visual movement not possible with individually sewn strips. The pattern and motif in a striped fabric generate unanticipated design variations. Finding a stripe fabric in an acceptable color scheme is often a shopping challenge, but the combination of striped fabric, design decisions, and "happy accidents" insures a unique mandala every time.

During my stint as clerk/teacher at a local quilt shop, I repeatedly saw competent, creative quilters become intimidated when it came to choosing fabric. Color choices are made by quilters who still do not view their skills as artistic talent. Often, they opt to defer to the color choices of a book, or to the "authority" behind the counter, and kits make it possible to skip over the color decisions. I discovered that striped fabrics are ready-made kits! They make it possible to make intricate, artistic mandalas without the hurdles of color choice and fabric arrangement, while still allowing you to maintain control of artistic decisions and design development.

The scavenger hunt for striped yardage is challenging but fun! Realize, before you shop for striped fabric, that all striped fabrics have printing inconsistencies due to the manufacturing process. Find an acceptable price tag for your budget. This is one time when paying more per yard does not necessarily yield a better quality stripe, because every stripe wavers to some extent.

In addition, those with repeating motifs have unequal distances between the motifs. How well we deal with these inconsistencies determines our success.

Striped fabrics are not common in most quilt shops, so expand your search to chain fabric houses and discount stores. Juvenile clothing or home decorator fabrics are a wonderful source of stripes. Decor fabrics are available in widths from 45 to 58 inches wide, which expands design possibilities. Although these are generally heavier than other fabrics, they work well. Decor cottons may be pricey, but they often contain additional repeats of stripes or motifs—they may actually be the better value.

DECODING STRIPES

Decoding means figuring out the specific characteristics of a particular striped fabric. It is one of the most interesting parts of making a mandala! Just like plaid fabrics, stripes can be even or uneven. They may have a "this end up" (one-way repeat) appearance. Stripes are printed either along the length (parallel) or across the length (perpendicular) of a fabric's grain. These

This folded back corner shows a one-way direction ("this end up") stripe.

stripes may contain large or small motifs.

Take a few minutes to look at the photos of completed quilts in the book. You'll notice narrow stripes, wide stripes, and rows of large-scale motifs (like roses and sunflowers). Some striped fabrics are plain, while others are extremely busy. Almost any striped fabric will work in any layout or design. Some designs just naturally lend themselves to a particular kind of stripe (i.e. pinwheels look great in wide stripes). Before you buy striped fabric, be sure to notice the color cross-section of fabric included with most of the quilt photographs. These will help give you a good idea of the stripes that work well in similar layouts. Caution: There are several exceptions to the "any stripe can be used" rule. The following can produce unpredictable, unreliable results: diagonally printed stripes, stripes that melt away then reappear, and stripes where the stripe is secondary to the motif.

When decoding, look for identical groupings of color or motif. These identical groupings are known as "sets," or for mandala purposes, "strata." Finding those identical groupings and identifying their directional quality is important. In some stripes the groupings are obvious (for example, awning or "prison" stripes), while in others, the groupings may be less obvious.

A border print is a variation of a stripe. In a border print, a wide, dominant motif is clustered parallel to the woven edge of one or both fabric edges. The area above (or between) the motif often has a subdued pattern or motif. Border prints can be used as strata. In a Bullseye design layout, a border print produces a wreath effect with an open central space (see Not Kansas Anymore, page 31).

Plaid fabric contains multiple intersecting stripes. Plaid fabric where only one side of the plaid dominates can be used as strata. In these plaids, colors are often more bold vertically than horizontally. These plaids are generally "uneven" and are often "this end up." Plaids produce dramatic arrows and cubes of color in Chevron design layouts.

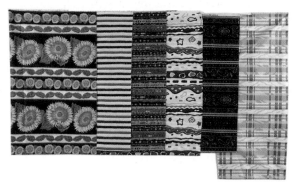

These three fabrics may have unreliable results. For instance, the plaid on the right is somewhat "watery." The fabric in the middle was successfully used for the quilt "Ripples," though.

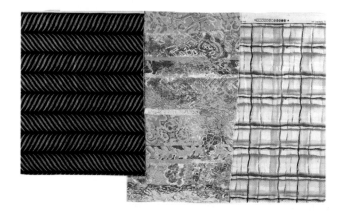

All of these are "good stripes." That is, they all have definite striped patterns (and they have all been successfully used in quilts).

These plaids do work as stripes!

A simple folding experiment will help decode the stripe. Look at the overall stripe. Which color or motif appears to jump out at you, or to be the most dominant? With right sides together, selvages parallel, match one dominant stripe to another laid directly on top of the first stripe. Fold back a corner from the selvage edge along a 45-degree (true bias) line. Do the dominant stripes continue to match in an arrow across the fold line? If all dominant stripes continue to match you have an even stripe. An uneven match signals an uneven stripe.

When decoding, it is also important to be aware of the size and placement of a motif. Motifs within a stripe are usually either stacked in vertical columns, checkerboard style, or staggered diagonally across the stripes. All motifs can be identical or there may be variations in the motif of alternate stripes. Motifs often have a "this end up" quality that requires one way (North, or wide, end up) cuts. It is important to note the size of a motif in comparison to the width of the wedge ruler in use. Will it fit within the seams of a single wedge? Must the motif be matched and seamed or will a wider wedge be used?

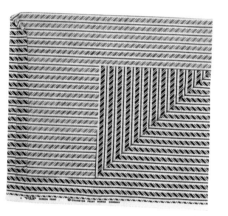

To test for an even stripe, fold on the lengthwise center, align the dominant stripes by peeking under the edges, and fold back a corner on a 45-degree/true bias line. If all of the dominant stripes match, it is an even stripe.

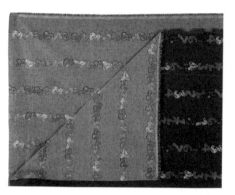

You can tell that this pattern has an even stripe when you fold back a corner.

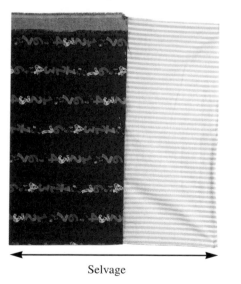

Selvage

The stripes are parallel to the selvage edge and are even.

Selvage

Stripes are either printed parallel (most common) or perpendicular to the woven selvage. These two fabrics are perpendicular to the woven selvage.

WHAT IF my motif is too large to fit within the seams of a single wedge?

A large floral or geometric motif is often what attracts you to a striped fabric. Retaining the motif's visual impact can be done by matching and piecing (invisible wedge) or by creating custom-sized wedge patterns. Wedge patterns can be made in any unique angle with the Original True Angle ruler or in multiples of the 9- or 15-degree rulers. Both methods require precision and additional yardage. Both can be auditioned in photocopy "dummies" before cutting fabric (see page 23).

In the invisible wedge method (see page 96), the motif is altered by its position along the North/South length of the ruler at cutting. In this method, reassembly of the motif with seams causes a downsizing or possible elimination of the motif.

In the wedge pattern method, the motif remains intact. In wedge patterns, some original seams are eliminated. Elimination of seams simplifies construction but will change the overall visual complexity of the medallion.

40 wedges down to 20 or 10 wedges: Double or Quad multi-wedge units

24 wedges down to 12 or 6 wedges: Double or Quad multi-wedge units

24 wedges down to 8 wedges: Triple multi-wedge units

Double, triple, and quad wedge patterns are made in tissue or dressmaker's pattern fabric. Several copies are cut in pattern fabric with the wedge ruler you are using. With accurate 1/4-inch seams, connect two, three, or four wedge patterns. Check the motif against the sewn multi-wedge pattern. Will the bulk of the motif be contained in a two-wedge pattern? Would the motif be better contained in a three (24 wedge, 15-degree ruler only) or four wedge pattern? Bullseye or Spoke design layouts will work with any multi-wedge pattern. The Chevron design layout will only work in multi-wedge patterns of two- or four-wedge units. Note: Petal or Pinwheel layouts are compromised by multiple wedge patterns that may not allow enough pieces for positioned repeats.

Does the chosen design layout use a straight or angled cutting position? Angled cutting positions are written on the wedge pattern, over the new vertical axis. These angles may or may not match the original angle markings on the wedge ruler you are using. In two- or four-wedge patterns, new angled positions are added to the patterns by drawing a 60- or 45-degree line intersecting the center seam (becomes the center vertical axis). In a three-wedge pattern, the center vertical axis occurs down the center of the middle wedge. That center can be found by matching the North/South raw edges of the center wedge and creasing before sewing or after sewing by matching sewn seams together pinning and creasing.

Seamed multi-wedge patterns are used like a dressmaker's pattern, pinned in position over prepared strata. A single pattern can be used to cut all multi-wedge units or several patterns can be prepared. Note: Care should be taken to not skim or stretch the pattern out of shape during use.

Here, a double-wide wedge "dummy" is used to cover the over-sized motif (the bunny).

Often, fabric is purchased because an over-sized motif is "attractive." That motif would be sliced beyond recognition in a single-wedge cut, and matching would require miles of yardage.

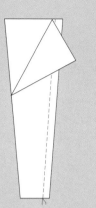

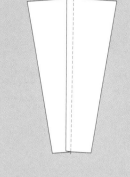

A single wedge cut in tissue paper or dressmaker's pattern paper.

Two tissue wedges.

Two wedges accurately seam at a scant 1/4 inch.

Double wedge pressed open (dry iron on medium heat); be careful not to leave any folds next to the seam.

Doubled pattern

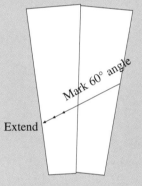

Mark 60° angle

Extend

Doubled wedges can be used for Sawtooth or Chevron (mirrored) cuts. The desired angle (45 or 60) should be marked on the doubled wedge in its original position on the right wedge. Then extend the marking across its partner. It will be slightly off from the original on the left wedge. Note that angles appear deeper and more exaggerated in doubled wedges than in single wedge cuts.

Bullseye layout with doubled wedge

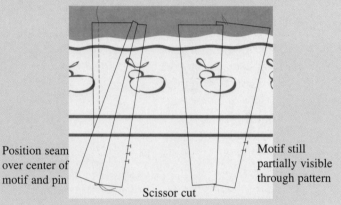

Position seam over center of motif and pin

Scissor cut

Motif still partially visible through pattern

Notice that due to the doubled wedge size that a motif will be skipped between each used.

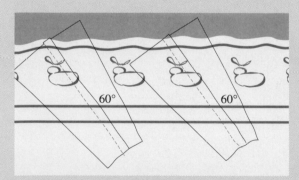

60°   60°

Position of doubled wedges for a Sawtooth layout.

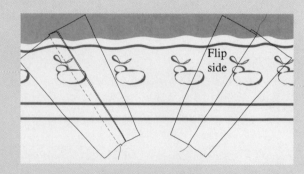

Flip side

Two layers of fabric can have right sides together or a single layer of right and left cuts (as shown here). This is the position of doubled wedges for a Chevron layout.

WHAT IF

after carefully calculating yardage I find a fabric flaw or a cut slips?

When yardage is limited this can either be a disaster or a happy accident. Here is a way to make it work, which was used in quilts pictured in this book. But in most instances, the "corrections" are not noticeable unless pointed out.

"Spare parts" are the waste at the beginning and at the end of each strata cut. These spare parts can fill the void of fabric shortages. These parts, when pieced to other remaining parts or short lengths of strata, are often enough to re-cut a wedge or two.

WHAT IF

all that remains of the strata is a small section not long enough for a whole wedge?

In any design, your eye seeks continuity, a connect-the-dots idea. Because of this and the natural visual movement in a mandala design, minor imperfections can easily be disguised. See if the remaining section of strata contains the dominant motif or color. Can a wedge be positioned over that section of strata so that the design flow is uninterrupted (i.e. the last drop match in a Pinwheel layout)? Additions of coordinate fabric or another stripe can be added above and/or below the dominant stripe. Because you have connected the dots, those add-ons are not obvious. If, after standing back to view this correction, it does stick out, consider putting a similar "correction" in several wedges positioned as highlights or spokes in the design.

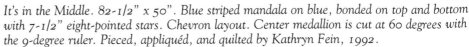

It's in the Middle. 82-1/2" x 50". Blue striped mandala on blue, bonded on top and bottom with 7-1/2" eight-pointed stars. Chevron layout. Center medallion is cut at 60 degrees with the 9-degree ruler. Pieced, appliquéd, and quilted by Kathryn Fein, 1992.

GUESSTIMATE YARDAGE

There is no precise method of calculating yardage for a mandala. I generally recommend a purchase of at least 6 yards of striped fabric for any mandala. Occasionally a mandala can be squeezed from as few as 4 yards, but that is rare.

Several factors determine the amount necessary for a mandala, but adequate yardage varies from stripe to stripe. Factors to consider include: the width/height of your stripe, the number of stripe repeats on the fabric, the length of the wedge being cut, and the angle that the wedge ruler is to be placed across the strata/stripe. There are a lot of variables!

Mandalas made with narrow, plain stripes will take less yardage than a mandala made from stripes with flowers or motifs to be matched or centered. The amount of waste, as well as overall yardage, needs to be considered "in the ballpark" and not an exact figure. Over-estimate and you won't be sorry; underestimating can result in some very creative juggling!

Guesstimates for large or dominant motifs can be slightly more exact. To guesstimate the needed yardage for large motifs, use several wedge rulers or cut tissue paper "dummies" of your wedge ruler. Each "dummy" wedge must be accurately cut with the 45- or 60-degree reference line clearly marked. Draw an outline of any motif to be centered onto the dummy. Position the wedge ruler in the desired location. Draw completely around the ruler with chalk or pencil, or lay a dummy wedge in position and secure it with a pin. Repeat the procedure at the next identical motif location on the strata. Continue this process until there are five identical dummies (six for the 15-degree wedge). (Note that the distances between wedge locations may be uneven.) On the strata, measure the furthest distance across those five dummies. Multiply that distance by 8 (or 4). This is the number of inches required. Divide the total by the number of strata repeats across the fabric (usually two or three times). This is a tight ballpark figure. Depending on the stripe you choose, you may need more than the general 6-yard guesstimate.

CHOOSING BACKGROUND FABRIC

Choosing fabric for the background of a mandala is an important decision. Its color and texture can enhance and add impact to your design or dilute all of your hard work. It is a decision that should be deferred until after your medallion is cut and sewn together. I have tons of yardage I purchased with striped fabric that was a coordinate print, or a collaborating color. Those fabrics should have been the perfect complement to the striped fabric I was using, but instead, when the mandala was placed on top, it looked flat, drained, dirty, and lifeless. This is very unexpected, but it seems that somewhere in the slice and dice of striped fabric into wedge-shaped pieces the design focus of the stripe shifts. What were originally the dominant colors and motifs are either diluted or compounded. Much like a kaleidoscope, it is practically impossible to anticipate what will occur until it does. (For more information on choosing a background fabric, see page 74.)

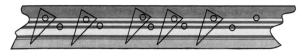

The sequence of five times the ruler dummies will be somewhat consistent throughout the yardage. The total distance across the wedges will also be consistent, but the distance between the dummies varies.

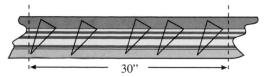

It takes 40 wedges for a full round and it takes eight repeats of those five wedge positions to equal a full round. So, 8 x 30 = 240" of strata (approx. 6-1/2 yards/rounded up to 7). This yardage figure is large because each yard of striped fabric usually contains at least two repeats of a stripe. The 7-yard total is divided by two striped (strata) repeats (7 ÷ 2 = 3.5 yards/rounded up to 4). So, the purchase of four yards of fabric would be adequate for this wedge ruler, in this position, on the stripe.

Standard mattress sizes vary by manufacturer. The following examples can be used for "in the ball park" estimates for design purposes. These measurements are the flat surface of the mattress and do not include an allowance for mattress thickness. Mattress thickness varies by style and on some "pillow top" models can be as deep as 12 inches, so measure yours to ensure a good fit.

Twin	39" x 75"	38" x 80"	36" x 72"
Full	54" x 75"	54" x 80"	53" x 72"
Queen	60" x 80"	60" x 80"	60" x 72"
King/Dual	76" x 80"		
Crib	27" x 52"	28" x 52-1/2"	
Day Bed	39" x 75"		

The 9° Circle Wedge Ruler in four sizes and the wedge extension. Photo courtesy Marilyn Doheny.

The original size of the 15-degree Wedge Ruler (left). This is the ruler that comes with the book Wedge Works (the ruler comes unmarked; the author marked this example for easier use). At right is the "Even Longer" Longer 15-degree Wedge.

*T*OOLS

When mandalas began, they were created with rulers, string, a compass, and the knowledge of geometry (which was considered sacred—a learned man's tool). When I began making quilted mandalas, the only rotary ruler available was the 9-degree wedge. Since then other wedge rulers, including the 15-degree and 11.5-degree, protractors, the Circle Slice ruler, and the Original True Angle have become available. While the tools vary slightly in their design and use, each is effective in mandala-making.

9° Circle Wedge Ruler: The wedge ruler is an ingenious tool designed to take the math mystery out of circle medallions. Created by Nancy Brister and marketed by Marilyn Doheny, the ruler evenly divides the 360 degrees of every circle into 40 equal wedge-shaped pieces of 9 degrees. The wedge ruler is made of transparent acrylic, with measured markings at inch increments and guidelines for both 45- and 60-degree design variations printed permanently on it. Quarter-inch seam allowances are marked on the sides. In this book "North" refers to the wide end of the ruler and "South" to the narrow end.

Measurements shown vertically down the ruler's center are radius measurements (one way out from center) and not the total distance across the medallion. Mandala medallions can be cut the full the length of any of the rulers or stopped short anywhere within its length. When 40 wedges are cut and sewn together, they form a doughnut-shaped medallion. The opening in the center will be approximately 6 inches in diameter. The ruler's measurements BEGIN at 3 inches. So all wedge pieces stop 3 inches BEFORE the center.

The 9° Circle Wedge Ruler is available in several sizes. The original ruler is 22 inches long and is used for mandalas up to 50 inches in diameter. An extension for the original wedge ruler is available to expand the diameter to 72 inches. The extension is especially useful for clothing or Christmas tree skirts. A variety package of "mini" wedges is also available. This package contains three wedge rulers that produce radii of 18, 14, and 9 inches. The shorter wedges are very easy to handle on narrow strata. These wedge rulers produce medallions for smaller projects such as wall hangings (36-, 28-, and 18-inch diameters).

15-degree Wedge Ruler: The 15-degree Wedge Ruler is another tool to make circle medallions. Cheryl Phillips developed this tool as an alternative to the 9-degree wedge. The 15-degree Wedge Ruler evenly divides the 360 degrees of every circle into 24 wedge-shaped pieces of 15 degrees each. The ruler is made of transparent acrylic and comes in several sizes. These sizes are convenient for block- or medallion-size circles. The wedge includes 1/4-seam allowances. But unlike the 9-degree ruler, this wedge ruler is unmarked. Reference points and angles for positioning are suggested via a template in Phillips' book, *Wedge Works*. Markings can be transferred to the ruler (see page 24). The book also includes templates to square out the corners of each standard size 24-wedge medallion.

With this ruler, 24 wedges are required to complete a full circle. When sewn together they form a doughnut-shaped medallion with a 2-inch diameter hole in the center. Design layouts with the 15-degree wedge are similar to those of the 9-degree wedge, however, some variation occurs because 24 is divisible by 2, 3, 4, 6, 8, and 12.

The Original True Angle is another tool for making circles. This adjustable protractor was developed for the building industry, but it has a multitude of uses for quilters. The Original True Angle was invented and marketed by Richard Quint. In his own custom cabinet shop, he found that there was no easy method for accurately and consistently making matching angles. This cost valuable time and money in remaking cabinets. The Original True Angle can create or duplicate any angle for wedge pattern making in seconds.

Made of lightweight, flexible, transparent plastic, it is marked in inches and centimeters. The Original True Angle has two blades that both rotate a full 360 degrees in either direction. Its center "hairline" is marked on

Different sizes of the Original True Angle.

both blades and locates an exact angle within 5/1000th tolerance. Quarter-inch seam allowances are located on one swing blade for pattern-marking convenience. An additional large numbered dial is available to make seeing the degree dial easy and accurate.

The Original True Angle is available in ten sizes to fit any design. The sizes most useful for mandala-making are the "shop" (23-5/8 x 2 inches) and "desk" (18 x 2 inches) sizes.

Rotary ruler, 6 x 24 inches: An acrylic ruler is a basic tool for rotary cutting. It provides an accurate 90-degree cut or check for perfect square corners. In the mandala process, this ruler is used when matching and layering lengths of stripes and/or motifs.

The Original True Angle set a 9 degrees with the over-sized dial attached.

Rotary cutter and mat: These are essential to assure accuracy not possible with scissors. The minimum size cutting mat for use with a 9-degree wedge is 18 x 24 inches, but 24 x 36 or a larger table-size mat is recommended. I recommend that you set up your cutting area on the open end of a wide, rectangular table or a kitchen counter peninsula. This provides comfortable access to two sides of your mat. You will be cutting from one side to another and will find it easier to physically move yourself as you cut. This approach improves accuracy and safety.

Sewing machine: Any well-maintained sewing machine can be used to construct a mandala. A simple straight stitch is all that is required for the initial construction.

Three different types of rotary cutters.

A variety of rotary cutting mats.

The stitch tension should be evenly balanced, top and bottom, with no pulling or distortion along a stitched seam line. In order to assure that the completed mandala lies flat, accurate 1/4-inch seams are essential. Variable needle positions can help in sewing a very accurate 1/4-inch seam. Adhesive or magnetic seam guides can reduce wavers along the seam's length. Zigzag and blind hem capabilities, while not essential, are a plus when it comes time to mount the medallion to a background.

Flat or "daisy head" straight pins: Careful alignment of several layers of striped fabric requires straight pins to anchor the layers together to prevent shifting. With daisy head pins, the wedge ruler lies perfectly flat over the pinned strata without the rocking that happens when regular straight pins are used under a rotary ruler, improving accuracy.

Wallpaper is an inexpensive and good way to practice wedge cutting techniques and accuracy. It has printing irregularities similar to those of fabric stripes—the distance between stripes can wobble and the space between motifs can be uneven. Miles of stripes in a double roll of paper provide plenty of play and design possibilities.

Photocopies: Some quilters prefer to experiment with several design options prior to cutting their fabric. Photocopies, when available, are helpful when choosing a design option or when yardage is limited. Copies eliminate the uncertainty of multiple design choices for those who do not like surprises. These gray and white wedge copies give a good indication of what kaleidoscope mutations will occur in fabric cut in the same positions. Multiple trial cuts in fabric chew up lots of yardage. Copies help cut down on lost yardage and aid accurate matches.

You'll need access to a copy machine that makes copies large enough for the strata to fit within the printing screen's measurement. Strata to be printed should be flat with no wrinkles. Do a trial copy. A good copy shows subtle variations in texture within each stripe as well as clearly showing motif outlines.

Several copies taped edge-to-edge will be necessary to simulate yardage. The copies can then be sliced with the wedge ruler and rotary cutter just like fabric. Remember, your wedge ruler includes 1/4-inch side seams. These should be skimmed off the photocopied wedges to give an accurate representation of a sewn unit. The skimmed seam copies will then be taped to each other to simulate a seam.

Photocopy wedges can be used as "dummies" to estimate yardage or as a substitute for "invisible" wedges (see Special Angles, page 98).

Sandpaper dots/strips: One of the many classroom discoveries was that sandpaper dots or strips applied to the back of the wedge ruler prevented much of the shifting and scooting of the ruler during rotary cutting. Sandpaper dots and strips stick like tape, but are not permanent and can be moved or removed if they interfere with reference lines or angles on the wedge ruler.

Tools for making crullers and fancy tips include: a small yellow French curve, a large fashion ruler (a dressmaker's French Curve), and a drafting snake (a flexible curve ruler).

Marking Wedges

Not all wedge tools have markings or labels. If your wedge ruler doesn't have them, I would recommend adding them yourself. Marking makes consistent placement of the ruler over striped fabric easy. Marking the wedge ruler can be done with a permanent pen, colored tape, exacto knife, or acrylic scribing tool. Of these tools, a permanent pen marking is the easiest to see, while the knife and scribing tool are the narrowest and most precise. All of these methods are permanent additions to your wedge ruler.

To mark your wedge ruler you will need a pen, paper, 6x12-inch straight-edge rotary ruler (with 45- and 60-degree marks), plus your marking tool. Begin by outlining your wedge ruler on the paper. Remove the wedge ruler. Measure, then mark, a 1/4-inch seam allowance on the narrow (South) end of the paper wedge. On the paper wedge measure, then mark, 1-inch increments along the length of the ruler. Be careful to keep the lines parallel to the seam line.

Design lines for angled layouts may also be added to the wedge. These angled lines can be at any angle to the 1-inch bars, but the most common are 45 and 60 degrees. Most 6x12-inch rotary rulers are marked with these angles. Align the angled line of the 6x12-inch ruler to one of the 1-inch bars. The edge of the ruler should fall within the wider part of the paper wedge. Follow the edge of the 6x12-inch ruler and mark that line on the paper wedge. If your 6x12-inch ruler does not have angle lines, drafting triangles are available in 30/60/90 and 45/90 in most office supply stores.

Return the wedge ruler to the paper wedge. Carefully position the ruler atop the paper pattern. To prevent sliding, use tape to secure the wedge over pattern. Using either your pen or scratching tool, transfer your seam allowance and 1-inch bars to the wedge ruler. Use a ruler to assure straight accurate lines. Transfer angled design lines as needed. Save the paper pattern for later additions to your wedge.

Drafting triangles and design line markings for marking paper wedge patterns or unmarked wedge rulers.

Making a Unique Angle Wedge

A mandala can be made with wedge shaped pieces of any angle. It is faster and easier to use standard ready-made wedge rulers, however the 360 degrees of any circle can be divided with a calculator into any degree wedge increments or combination of wedge increments. The easiest wedges to make are those wedges that have degree numbers that evenly divide 360 degrees. Those even divisions result in whole numbers without any extra fractions or decimal remainders. For example, 360 divided by 6 = 60 (6 wedges of 60 degrees each), or 6 combinations of 45 degrees + 15 degrees.

Elaborate mathematical or technical drafting formulas were once the only way to get wedge-shaped pieces of a circle. The half moon-shaped protractors were an easier, but not always accurate, solution to wedge-shaped pieces. Recently an adjustable dual blade tool, the Original True Angle, has made accurate custom angles effortless.

To make wedge-shaped patterns with the Original True Angle you will need a pen or very sharp pencil, a large sheet of paper, dressmaker's pattern fabric, or template plastic, and either a shop- or office-size Original True Angle. First make a long, straight line 1 inch from the edge. There is a screw at the intersection of the two blades. Loosen the screw and allow the blades to swing easily in either direction. Do not remove the screw or separate the blades. In the center of each blade is a "hairline" marking. Position that center marking over the straight line on the paper. To prevent slipping, tape that blade to your paper. Examine the numbered dial that connects the blades at the screw. The numbers are full degrees of a circle. Align the "hairline" of the second blade with the degree number chosen. Exact alignment is important. Tighten the screw. Draw a line along the edge of the second blade. Release the tape, but do not loosen the screw holding blades. Using a ruler or the long edge of the Original True Angle, connect the lines in a pie-shaped piece.

Position the inner edges of the Original True Angle over the pie-shaped marking. Check for accuracy. The point of the pie is the center of the circle. Because of the difficulty in sewing many evenly intersecting seams, mandalas pieces do not go all the way to the center of the circle. They are shortened to a wedge shape. Measure 2 inches from the point up both sides of the pie. Connect those points with a straight line. This is the South edge of your new wedge pattern. This wedge pattern can be any length. With a ruler, measure from the South edge on both legs of the pie, then connect the dots for the North/top edge of the wedge pattern.

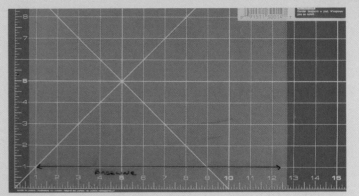

The long, straight "baseline" is made 1 inch from the edge of the template plastic.

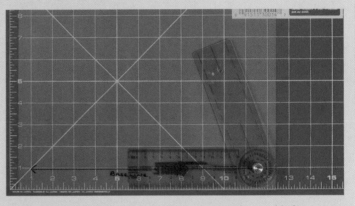

The Original True Angle's screw is loosened so its blades can swing freely.

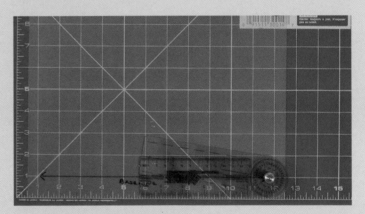

The bottom blade's "hairline" is positioned over the straight line on the template plastic while the upper blade's "hairline" is set at the chosen degree mark.

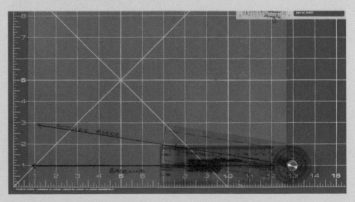

The lines are connected into a pie-shaped piece.

Handles: Another classroom revelation was the use of rotary ruler handles on the wedge ruler. Some students recommended suction handles to equalize pressure on the wedge during cutting and to move their fingers away from the rotary blade. These suction-mounted holders come as knobs or handles and can easily be moved or removed.

Extra hands: An extra pair of eyes and hands is a big help in the mandala process. They can match miles of stripe with teamwork and piles of flat head straight pins. In the classroom, students benefited from having multiple minds to notice and correct construction problems and multiple hands to tape, mount, and pin-baste each medallion to its background.

French curve (dressmaker's curve): This is a tool for making a variety of arcs (curves) generally used in garment patterns. This tool is also useful in connecting wedges of uneven lengths in smooth arcs, or making rounded petal-shaped wedge tips. French curves are made in metal, plastic, and acrylic, and come in a variety of sizes. For mandala purposes, a 12- to 16-inch size is the most convenient.

Protractor: This is a tool for measuring and marking angles. Its half-moon shape is divided into 180 degree increments. The degrees are marked along the curved edge of the moon shape. For ease of left and right facing angles, protractors are often marked both left to right and right to left (1-180degrees and 180-1degrees). They are made of metal, plastic, and acrylic, and are available in many sizes. Some protractors contain a swing arm for repeating angles or checking an angle's accuracy.

Protractors were the only way to divide a circle into degrees before wedge rulers and the Original True Angle.

Template Plastic: This is used for making wedge-shaped patterns or pattern dummies. Made of a stiff translucent material, it comes in several thicknesses and colors. It can be plain or gridded like graph paper. Template plastic can be marked with a pen or permanent marker, and it can be cut and shaped with regular household scissors.

A variety of template plastic; any of these can be used for making patterns for special angle wedges, marking an unmarked wedge ruler, or double-wide wedge patterns.

For My Friends. Multi-layout sampler. This quilt "was an experiment with the ruler and fabrics to see how many different combination of wedges I could come up with. Each fan was dedicated to a member of the Mandala Class and Sheila." Its "sister" quilts are Friendship Flower and Friendship Knot (see pages 50 and 98, respectively). Machine pieced and quilted by Sue Gerbick.

Chapter *4*

ESIGN DIARY

While magic mandalas may look intricate, there are actually only two standard layouts: straight and angled. In straight layouts, the ruler is placed straight across the stripes. These layouts include the Bullseye, Pinwheel, Swirl, Petal, Sunburst, Split Tip, and Spokes. In angled layouts, the ruler is placed at a 45- or 60-degree angle to the stripe. These layouts include the Sawtooth, Chevron, and combination layouts.

Definitions and examples of each layout and its variations are illustrated in this chapter. The illustrations are shown in the same black and white strata. While the repetition of this basic stripe seems monotonous, it reinforces the versatility of the mandala menu. Any stripe can be used in any recipe! Do not allow color to distract you from the design characteristics of a layout—the color of a stripe is bonus, a secondary consideration. It imparts a mood but does not change the characteristics of any design layout. Study the layout charts. Observe how the ruler looks positioned over the stripe. See how that wedge position looks as a single wedge. See how two wedges look together, then four, then more. Both straight and angled layouts may be combined to produce even more variation. These combinations require more than one cutting position.

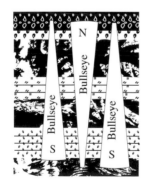

Straight cut

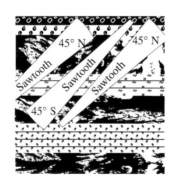

Angled cut

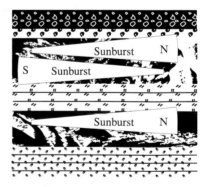

Straight cut

FLOWCHART

The following flowchart illustrates the design possibilities of each layout.

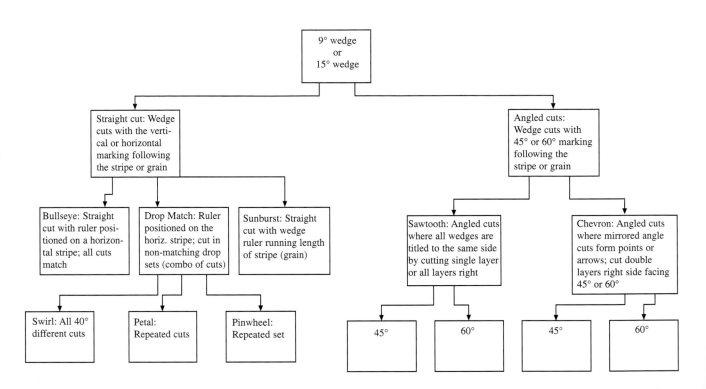

9° wedge
or
15° wedge

Straight cut: Wedge cuts with the vertical or horizontal marking following the stripe or grain

Angled cuts: Wedge cuts with 45° or 60° marking following the stripe or grain

Bullseye: Straight cut with ruler positioned on a horizontal stripe; all cuts match

Drop Match: Ruler positioned on the horiz. stripe; cut in non-matching drop sets (combo of cuts)

Sunburst: Straight cut with wedge ruler running length of stripe (grain)

Sawtooth: Angled cuts where all wedges are titled to the same side by cutting single layer or all layers right

Chevron: Angled cuts where mirrored angle cuts form points or arrows; cut double layers right side facing 45° or 60°

Swirl: All 40° different cuts

Petal: Repeated cuts

Pinwheel: Repeated set

45°

60°

45°

60°

WHAT IF the design is more than a single wedge short? Is making a fan the only option?

Examine your options. Spare parts or unused South cuts may be the answer. Often a length of stripe was stripped out between the strata used. That stripe may have been reserved as borders or just considered waste. This happened in "Tilting at Pinwheels." I had removed the "wimpy" blue from the other strong stripe colors. Then I found I was three wedges short with the source of the fabric 600 miles away! To complete the final wedge of each of the five blades, I resurrected that blue stripe. The blue stripe was cut at an odd angle (because that was how I could get all five blades out). Suddenly it became the focusing element for the pinwheel shape and the highlight color for that mandala!

In "Floral Fan" the fabric was down to threads and there still wasn't enough. A peach ribbon stripe remained in slivers. Those slivers were pieced together with 1/8 inch seams (or less) and added to the vertical edges of several wedges. The wedges were then trimmed to shape. The slivers became "mini" spokes placed evenly through the fan.

Tilting at Pinwheels' perimeter extension with shaped edges.

Spare fabric parts make mini spokes in Floral Fan.

DESIGN DEFINITIONS
STRAIGHT LAYOUTS

BULLSEYE: A familiar archery symbol. It consists of several concentric circles occurring at roughly equal distances from each other. The Bullseye is the simplest straight-cut mandala. It bends a motif or pattern within each stripe into a curve. These curves are amazingly versatile used as pieces or parts. Parts of a Bullseye can frame, border, or combine with spacers to create chain links, tendrils, or fretwork.

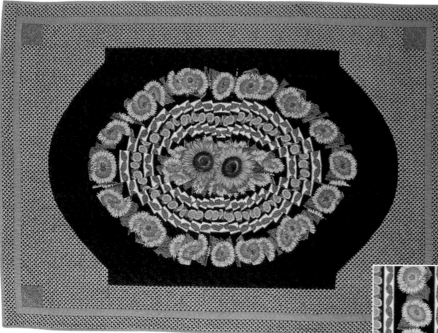

Sunflower. Approx. 45" x 60". Yellow/gold/blue on navy. Bullseye layout in measured lengths working from the perimeter toward the center. The flowers were carefully repieced. An over-sized cheater panel was center-fused and needle-darned in position. The border is "tavern sign" style. Designed, pieced, and quilted by Sheila Finklestein.

Not Kansas Anymore. Approx. 80" x 90". Pink/green/black on black gingham. Bullseye layout using a Daisey Kingdom border print. This quilt has a loose "petal" edge perimeter. Designed and pieced by Sheila Finklestein. Quilted by Sheila Finklestein and Helen Wiley.

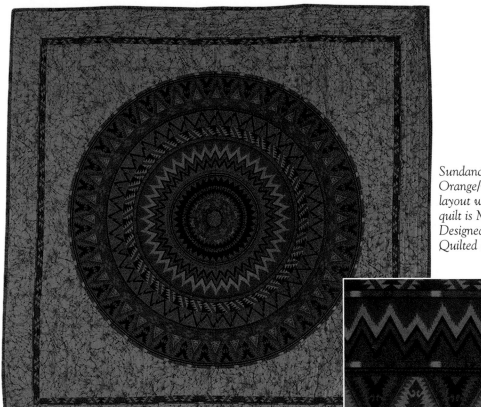

*Sundance. Approx. 60" x 60".
Orange/red/magenta on orange. Bullseye
layout with an eight-patch center. Its "sister"
quilt is Medicine Wheel (see page 5).
Designed and pieced by Sheila Finklestein.
Quilted by Debby Lee.*

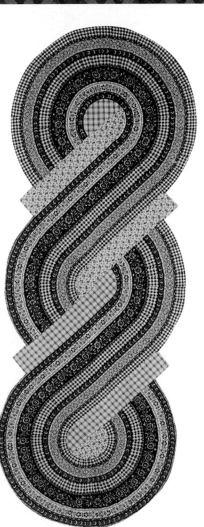

*Right: Country Lane. Approx. 22" x 72".
Red/blue/green. Bullseye layout with multiple
medallions. Designed, pieced, and quilted by
Sheila Finklestein.*

*Above: Kelly green spacers
in Interlocken go into the
centers.*

9-degree wedge (40)
Bullseye

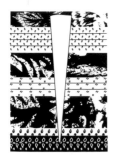

The ruler should be
placed perpendicular
or at a right angle to
the stripe.

A single
wedge; these
may be cut in
multiple
layers.

A pair; care-
fully-cut
stripes will
align at the
seams.

Two pairs of wedges

Ten wedges (a quarter round)

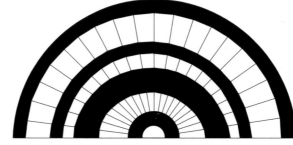

Twenty wedges (a half round)

15-degree
wedge (24)
Bullseye

The ruler should be
placed perpendicular
or at a right angle to
the stripe.

A single wedge;
these may be cut
in multiple layers.

A pair; carefully-cut
stripes will align at
the seams

Quarter round (6)

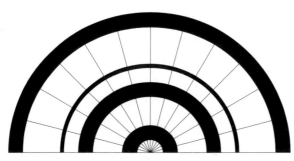

Half round (12)

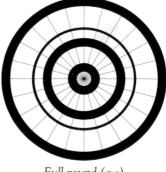

Full round (24)

9-degree wedge (40)
Bullseye plus spoke

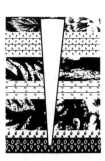

Single wedge ruler
placement.

Single-wedge
Bullseye.

Mirror cuts

A single-wedge
Chevron forms the
spokes.

Two wedge
pairs

Two wedge
pairs; this shows
spoke structure.

Two wedge pairs;
this does not show
unit structure yet.

Ten wedges (a quarter round) with one half
Chevron unit at each end. Here, the spokes
begin; the strata will not align to the previous
strata/stripe.

Twenty wedges (a half round). Spokes form at quarter
points.

DESIGN DEFINITIONS
STRAIGHT LAYOUTS (CONT.)

PINWHEEL: A classic design symbol, suggesting the whirling, perpetual movement of a child's toy. The Pinwheel layout is similar to the Bullseye in that each wedge is straight-cut, perpendicular to the stripe. However, the Pinwheel is a "drop match." That is, the position across the stripe is staggered or "dropped" some distance either lower or higher than it appeared in the previous wedge cut. In a Pinwheel, those "drops" occur in repeating groups or sets of cuts, and the combination of drops forms the "blades" of the Pinwheel. The blades of a Pinwheel are usually of equal sizes. Each blade must be an even division of the 40 or 24 wedges full round. Because we are dealing with numbers that evenly divide a circle, several variations of the Pinwheel exist.

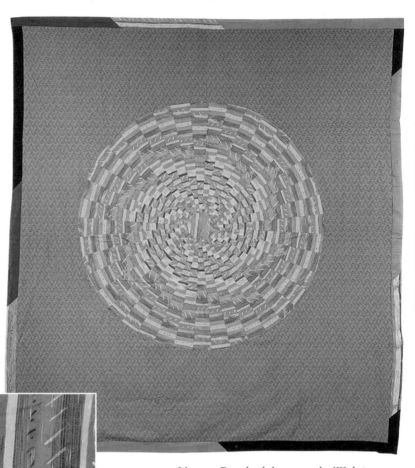

Vortex. Pinwheel drop match. With its swirling pattern of pastel hues, this quilt seems to move as in Webster's Dictionary's definition: "A whirling mass drawings objects to a central cavity." Machine pieced by Cathy Jackson.

PINWHEEL VARIATIONS FOR 40 WEDGE MANDALA (9-DEGREE WEDGE RULER)

NUMBER OF WEDGES IN BLADE	NUMBER OF BLADES
2	20
4	10
5	8
8	5
10	2

PINWHEEL VARIATIONS FOR 24 WEDGE MANDALA (15-DEGREE WEDGE RULER)

NUMBER OF WEDGES IN BLADE	NUMBER OF BLADES
2	12
3	8
4	6
6	4
8	3
12	2

Tilting at Pinwheels. Approx. 75" x 75". Red/black/green/blue on crayon yellow. Drop-match layout with spokes. It has perimeter extensions from spare parts and a five-patch center. Designed, pieced, and quilted by Sheila Finklestein.

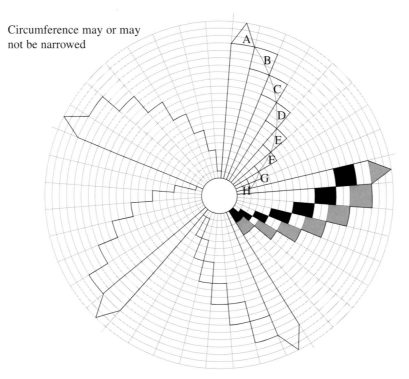

9-degree wedge five-blade Pinwheel (eight wedge sets) with a one-way drop.

Celestial Spin. 45" diameter circle wall hanging. Drop-match Pinwheel layout done on an angle. Designed, pieced, and quilted by Cindy Scott, 1995.

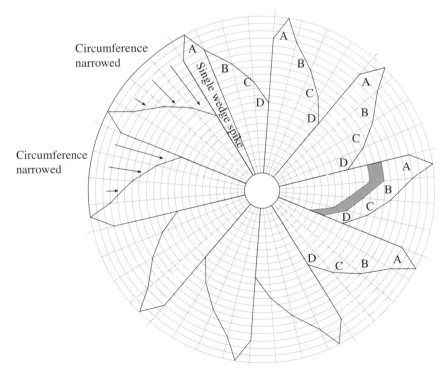

9-degree wedge ten-blade Pinwheel (five wedge sets)

PINWHEEL VARIATIONS FOR 9-DEGREE WEDGE

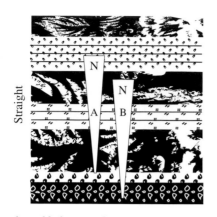

Straight

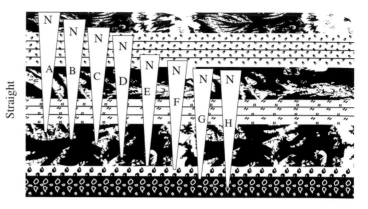

Straight

Pinwheel with 20 blades straight cut. For a two-position Pinwheel, cut 20 repeats (blades) of the set shown. Cut a single layer or all faceup. Label the positions (A, B, C, etc.) and assemble them in order. The strata will not match—it will "drop."

For an eight-position Pinwheel, cut five repeats of the set shown. Cut a single layer or all faceup. Label the positions (A, B, C, etc.) and assemble them in order. The strata will not match—it will "drop."

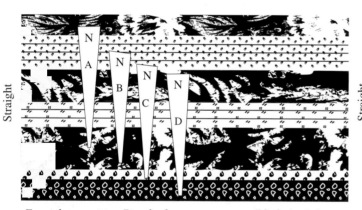

Straight

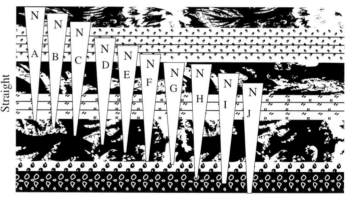

Straight

For a four-position Pinwheel, cut ten repeats (blades) of the set shown. Cut a single layer or all faceup. Label the positions (A, B, C, etc.) and assemble them in order. The strata will not match—it will "drop."

For a ten-position Pinwheel, cut four repeats (blades) of the set shown. Cut a single layer or all faceup. Label the positions (A, B, C, etc.) and assemble them in order. The strata will not match—it will "drop."

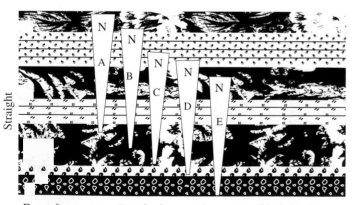

Straight

For a five-position Pinwheel, cut eight repeats (blades) of the set shown. Cut a single layer or all faceup. Label the positions (A, B, C, etc.) and assemble them in order. The strata will not match—it will "drop."

DESIGN DEFINITIONS
STRAIGHT LAYOUTS (CONT.)

SWIRL: Like the Pinwheel, the Swirl uses a drop-match placement. In a Swirl, however, **every** wedge is dropped and requires a different placement across the stripe. Forty (or twenty-four) unique positions require an unusually wide strata to accomplish it without duplicating wedge positions. It should be noted that the Swirl layout has a definite stop and start wedge. It is unlikely that those points visually connect.

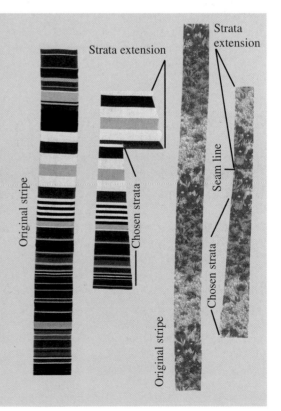

Rollout. Approx. 50" x 50". Acid to apple green on celadon. Swirl 40-position angle drop-match layout. Both North and South cuts were used for this quilt which has wedge-rounded corners. Spare parts were combined into a mille-wedge center. Designed, pieced, and quilted by Sheila Finklestein.

Spring Spin. Approx. 50" x 50". Medium pastels on lavender. Swirl 40-degree position, straight drop-match layout. Designed and pieced by Sheila Finklestein. Quilted by Debby Lee.

WHAT IF

I want to do a 40- (or 24-) position Swirl design layout but the strata repeat is not "deep enough?"

Add on to the widest stripe (or the stripe that you want to dominate). The "add-on" is a duplicate stripe or set of stripes seamed onto the original fabric yardage to allow for more cutting positions. Add it adjacent to where the stripe originally occurred (i.e. lavender stripe in Spring Spin) making it appear wider—easy cutting add-ons work best added to either the North or the South of a strata strip. They can be sewn in one or several positions as needed, though. Note: Add-ons in mid-strata require a longer duplicate stripe because that add-on will occur in most wedge cutting positions.

Some mandala layouts require an unusually deep strata repeat. Reasons to extend strata include: a Swirl (40 separate cutting positions, i.e. the quilt Spring Swirl), a cross grain printed stripe limits the width of the strata, and a previously cut strata for a second or revised design (i.e. the quilt Hurricane). Adding an extension should be subtle and non-jarring. You can do this by widening an existing stripe combination (Hurricane), or by doubling up on the width of a favorite or dominant color (Spring Swirl).

Strata extension

Strata extension

Original stripe

Chosen strata

Seam line

Chosen strata

Original stripe

DESIGN DEFINITIONS
STRAIGHT LAYOUTS (CONT.)

PETAL: Another variation of the straight-cut, drop-match layout. Petals suggest something floral; they are cut in groups of wedges, like a Pinwheel. In a Pinwheel every wedge of a blade has its own "drop," whereas in a Petal, "drop" may be done in repeats or mirrored cuts. (A/B/C/B/A or A/B/C/Bm/Am). Mirrored cuts are separated and arranged into right and left sides of each Petal. Each Petal equals a whole group or set. Each group is an even division of 40 (or 24) wedges full round. Just as there are several variations of the Pinwheel, there are several variations of the Petal layout.

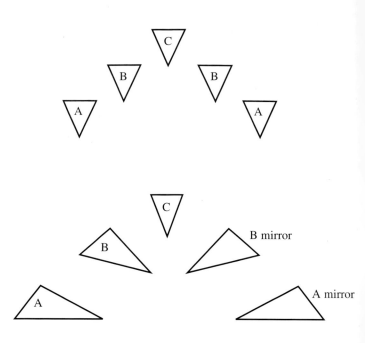

Sequence of the positions. In this five-position sequence the "A" and "B" positions either appear twice or the "A" and "B" positions appear once with a mirror of A and B and Am and Bm coming as the repeat.

PETAL VARIATIONS FOR 40 WEDGE MANDALA (9-DEGREE WEDGE RULER)	
NUMBER OF WEDGES PER PETAL	NUMBER OF PETALS
2	20
4	10
5	8
8	5
10	4

PETAL VARIATIONS FOR 24 WEDGE MANDALA (15-DEGREE WEDGE RULER)	
NUMBER OR WEDGES PER PETAL	NUMBER OF PETALS
2	12
3	8
4	6
6	4
8	3
12	2

Miracle Grown. Approx. 54" x 70". Pale pastels on mottled yellow/blue. Petal drop-match layout. Designed, pieced, and quilted by Sheila Finklestein.

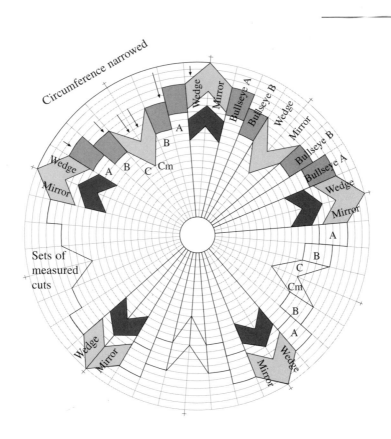

9-degree wedge (40) five petals (eight wedge set) with four long mirrored spokes or pairs, four short mirrored pairs, ten A Bullseye wedges, and ten B Bullseye wedges.

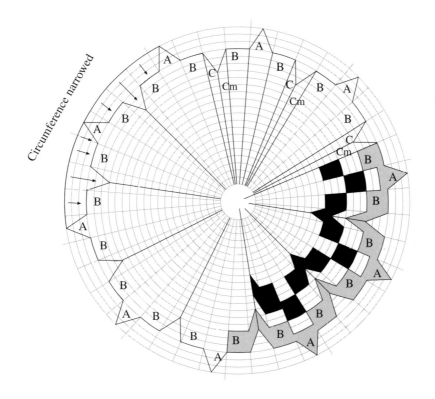

9-degree wedge (40) ten petals of four wedge sets (ten A wedges, 20 B Bullseye wedges, ten C split (C and C mirrored). A similar layout was used in Miracle Grown (see opposite page).

DESIGN DEFINITIONS
STRAIGHT LAYOUTS (CONT.)

SUNBURST: A straight-cut layout where the long centerline of the wedge ruler falls directly along the dominant design stripe. This forms a long, narrow, repeated spike at each seam line with the center of each wedge radiating strongly outward. This layout suggests sunshine or starlight pouring out on a child's drawing. The visual effect is of growth or expansion.

SPLIT TIP: This is a version of the Sunburst. A Split Tip is created when an extra-wide stripe is centered vertically, equally dividing the wedge along its centerline. The many vertical lines created with this layout suggest explosive movement.

SUNBURST VARIATION: Realigning the dominant design stripe to fall along one edge of the wedge ruler produces the illusion of rolling movement. When all layers are cut face-up, this slight angling gives a visual twist similar to the multiple spokes of a bicycle tire. When cut as mirrored pairs (right sides together), this Sunburst variation will create deeper dagger-like arrows at one seam line and a dominant vertical ray when sewn to its neighbors. This variation works well for large motifs. The cut angles through mid-stripe rescales the original motif, creating clusters of motifs at the outer doughnut and smaller motifs as they near the doughnut hole. Rescaling is very dramatic when used as a spoke.

Road to Candyland. Approx. 60" x 80". Orange/blue/yellow on white. Split Tip layout. This quilt has multiple quarter rounds in a snail trail design unit and double wedge-mitered tips. Designed and pieced by Sheila Finklestein. Quilted by Helen Wiley.

War Bonnet. 50" diameter wall hanging. Sunburst layout. Created from a single striped fabric. Designed, machine pieced, and quilted by Pat Marshall.

DESIGN DEFINITIONS

STRAIGHT LAYOUTS
(CONT.)

SPOKES: A method of using the Sunburst cut wedge to highlight, disperse, or break up the monotony of some designs. Spokes are used as visual punctuation. They can be either a single wedge or multiple wedges. The stripe usually falls along the longest vertical line, the center vertical, although other angles are sometimes used. Spokes are generally evenly distanced from each other, as in a gear or wheel. The most common number of spokes are four or five in a 9-degree mandala (three or four in a 15-degree mandala). Spokes are often longer or employ an alternate-shaped tip to further emphasize their position. Mirrored pairs of wedges can be used for spokes. Spokes can be used to rescue a layout when yardage is inadequate.

This spoke from the Medicine Wheel shows a perimeter finished edge

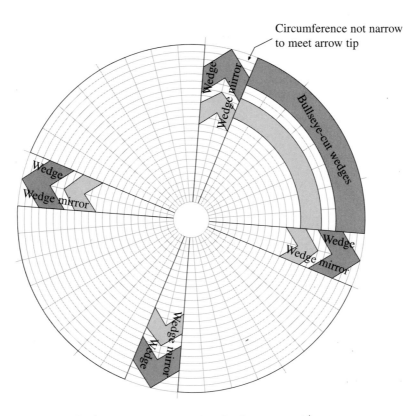

Spokes. Four mirror wedges (with arrow tips).

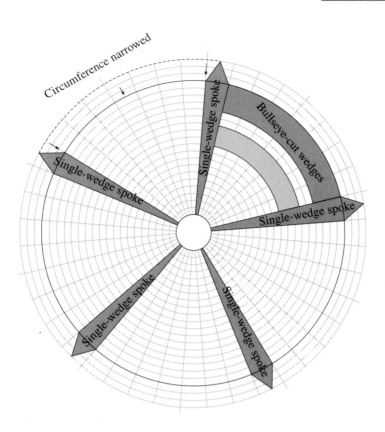

Spokes. Five single spikes, or spokes, evenly spaced.

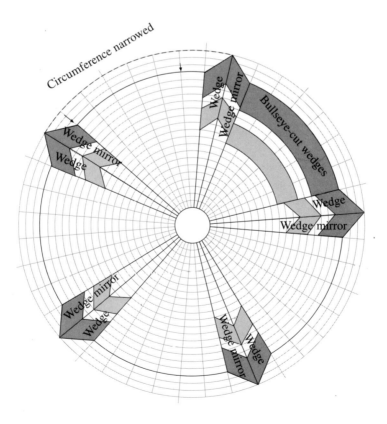

Spokes. Five mirrored double wedges with arrow tips.

DESIGN DEFINITIONS
ANGLED LAYOUTS

SAWTOOTH: It results when the printed junction of the stripe is placed on or parallel to either the 45- or 60-degree markings of the wedge ruler. In a Sawtooth, these cuts are made in a single layer (or all face-up) with the identical angle across the identical stripe. Stripe "seams" are offset from their position in the previous wedge and will not align to those of the previous wedge when sewn to their neighbors. Motifs are sliced beyond recognition in a Sawtooth, so the resulting mandalas are textural with few recognizable motif shapes. The blur of motif reinforces the effect of swift visual spin in this layout.

Hurricane.
Approx.
45" x 36".
Blue/yellow/red/white on navy. Sawtooth layout. The four-patch center is the nautical symbol for a hurricane, and the overall shape of the medallion is the meteorological symbol for hurricane. Designed, pieced, and quilted by Sheila Finklestein.

Frantic. Approx. 108" x 108". Kelly green/red/navy on white. 45-degree Sawtooth layout. The medallion is 72" and was made with the 9° Circle Wedge Ruler extension. The quilt has lattice corners. Its "sister" quilt is Fiesta (see page 55). Designed and pieced by Sheila Finklestein. Quilted by Sheila Finklestein and Debby Lee.

9-degree wedge (40)
60-degree Sawtooth

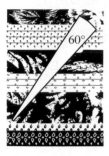

Position the ruler over the stripe. For the Sawtooth layout, wedges are cut in a single layer or all layers faceup.

Single wedge

Pair of wedges

Two pairs

Ten wedges (a quarter round)

Twenty wedges (a half round)

15-degree wedge (24)
60-degree Sawtooth

Single wedge

Pair of wedges

Quarter round (6)

Half round (12)

Full round (24)

9-degree wedge (40)
45-degree Sawtooth

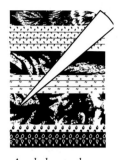    

Angled cut, the 45-degree Sawtooth. Position the ruler over the stripe. For the Sawtooth layout, the wedges are cut in a single layer or all layers faceup.

A single-cut wedge

A pair; the printed pattern will not line up at the seam lines.

Two pairs

Ten wedges (a quarter round)

Twenty wedges (a half round). Note the dramatic "chop" within the stripe position.

15-degree wedge (24)
60-degree Sawtooth

Single wedge

Pair of wedges

Quarter round (6)

Half round (12)

Full round (24)

DESIGN DEFINITIONS

ANGLED LAYOUTS (CONT.)

CHEVRON: Like the Sawtooth, the stripe is positioned on or parallel to either the 45- or 60-degree markings of the wedge ruler, but the Chevron is made with mirrored cuts. Wedges are cut in a carefully-matched layer of strata, right sides together. The multiple mirrored pairs create connecting arrows that ripple their way around the doughnut in a roller coaster effect. The visual ripples produced by 60-degree cuts are graceful and rolling. The rippled effect of 45-degree cuts are sharper, with dramatic spiked angles. The mirror angled cuts create additional secondary designs. These secondary designs are kaleidoscope-like mutations of the original motif.

Russet Fans. Approx. 45" x 54". Rust/red/brown/on cream. 60-degree Chevron layout. This quilt was laid-out as quarter round fans (North cuts on one side and South cuts opposite); this took 2 yards of very careful cutting. The perimeter has sewn mitered tips. Unquilted. Designed and pieced by Sheila Finklestein.

Green Fantom. Approx. 45" x 60". Pink/purple/yellow on kelly green. 45-degree Chevron. Both North and South cuts were used as opposing fans. Its "sister" quilt is Sunny's Day (see page 81). Designed and pieced by Sheila Finklestein. Owned by Mikey J. Markel.

Friendship Flower. 30" square wall hanging. 45-degree Chevron. Its "sister" quilts are For My Friends and Friendship Knot (see pages 28 and 98, respectively). Pieced and quilted by Cindy Scott, 1994.

9-degree wedge (40)
45-degree Chevron

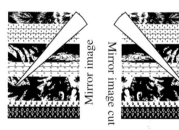

45 Chevron, two-layer cut.

A pair formed from one
wedge or each cut.

Carefully-cut pairs
will match and form
arrows.

Two pairs, two from
each cut, with their
partners.

Ten wedges (a quarter round);
five partnered pairs.

Twenty wedges (a half round); ten partnered pairs.

15-degree wedge (24)
60-degree Chevron

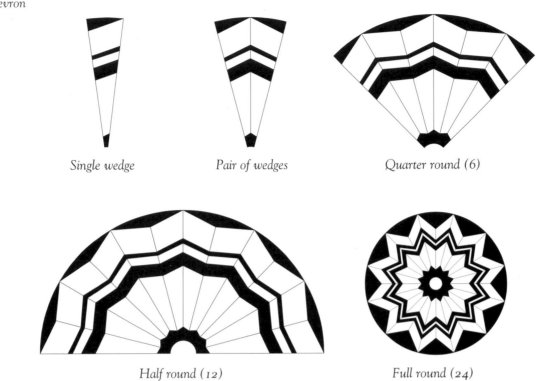

Single wedge   Pair of wedges   Quarter round (6)

Half round (12)   Full round (24)

Note the difference between the gentle ripple of 60 degrees and the dramatic arrows of 45 degrees.

15-degree wedge (24)
45-degree Chevron

Single wedge   Pair of wedges   Quarter round (6)

Half wedge (12)   Full round (24)

Lace and Stars. 87" x 87". Blue/white on dark blue. Chevron layout. This 50" light-colored mandala is surrounded by a border of 36 eight-pointed starts. The back has the same mandala as the front, but it was cut into quarters and off-set from the edge by six eight-pointed stars. Pieced and quilted by Sydna L. Herren-Freund.

*H*OW TO: MAKING A MANDALA

Chapter 5

THE BASIC RULES

Now that you have some background on fabrics, tools, and different layouts, you are ready to begin making your mandala. There are basic guidelines to consider for all stages of mandala construction. These rules are presented by their phase of construction: fabric, positioning the ruler, sewing and pressing, finishing, and quilting. Review these basics before you begin each project.

FABRIC RULES

❶ Always buy more fabric than needed.
❷ Ignore the woven grain line in printed stripes.
❸ Cut strata with scissors.
❹ Cut wedges with a rotary cutter.

SEWING/PRESSING RULES

❶ Be sure your cutting and sewing skills are accurate and consistent.
❷ Use the South end of wedges as reference points for match wedges. Do not slide wedge positions (retrim when necessary).
❸ Begin all seams at the South end of wedges.
❹ Seam in pairs, quarter rounds, and then halves.
❺ Dry iron only (no steam) until final seams are in.
❻ Press all seams to the same side.

POSITIONING RULES

❶ Be consistent in lining up reference lines and points on the ruler and within the stripe.
❷ Always mark your ruler with tape, or write reminder notes for the location of reference points (i.e. 60-degree angle "top of the wide yellow stripe").
❸ Be sure the South (narrow) end of ruler always falls completely within bounds of strata used.
❹ Be sure the South end of wedge cuts are evenly trimmed.
❺ The North (wide) end of ruler may overhang strata used (overhang should be consistent).
❻ Pin the dominant stripe or motif to the same stripe in the strata layer below.
❼ Check motif and stripe alignment (retrim wedge when necessary).
❽ Lay multi-position layouts next to machine in the order they are to be stitched.

FINISHING RULES

❶ Audition several centers.
❷ Audition several background fabrics with the completed medallion.
❸ Anchor medallion to background with lots of straight pins.
❹ Appliqué with close stitches and double-stitch any points.
❺ Add borders.

QUILTING RULES

❶ Remove background fabric from under medallion if hand-quilting only.

❷ Layer quilt sandwich.

❸ Baste (hand or pin) closely over mandala to prevent bunching and scooting while quilting.

❹ Begin all quilting near the center of the mandala and work outward.

❺ Balance the quilting in the mandala and background areas.

❻ Avoid close concentric quilting in the center 12 inches of the mandala (this can cause the quilt to bunch up like a drawstring purse).

PREPARE THE STRIPE

Because stripes are printed on fabric, striped lines do not always parallel the fabric's woven grain lines. To prepare an easily usable length of stripe (strata) it is necessary to separate it from the length of fabric yardage. "Strip out the strata" is the separation of the desired stripe repeats from the length of yardage. Stripes cannot be ripped along the yardage or cut with a rotary cutter. Stripping the strata away from the original yardage must be done with scissors; this provides narrow strata units. It is easier to align directional stripes and motifs for multiple layer cuts with narrow strata. Narrow strata simplifies wedge lengths and unifies "over-cut" tips.

PIN LAYERING

This is the matching of stripes and motifs with pins prior to cutting wedges. After stripping the strata away from the original yardage, two layers of strata are aligned motif to identical motif. Straight pins are used to anchor the layers together. The straight pins should have small or flat flower heads. Small or flat head pins allow the ruler to lie directly on top without causing it to rock or slide. Sliding is both an accuracy and a safety issue.

Layering can be done alone or with another quilter. Layers are aligned as either matching (all one side up) or mirrored cuts (two sides facing each other). Dominant stripes are aligned and the first motif matched. Hold the layers apart like the blades of a scissors (partner's job). Lay a 6 x 24-inch straight ruler across the matched doubled strata. Align one of the ruler's horizontal markings to the lengthwise cut edge of the strata. Following that edge, slide the ruler along the doubled strata length. As the strata come together with the weight of the ruler, check, then pin, each

motif match. Motif match is checked by pulling the strata back (the "scissors blades") against the straight edge every time the ruler is midway across a motif. If the motif of one strata does not align with the motif of another strata, match the motif, then allow the strata to buckle between the cutting positions. Repeat the slide and match process for each set of strata.

CONSTRUCTION

The construction of a mandala actually begins before you use your sewing machine. Construction of a mandala includes the cutting of wedges, the organization of cuts, and the sewing and pressing of wedge units.

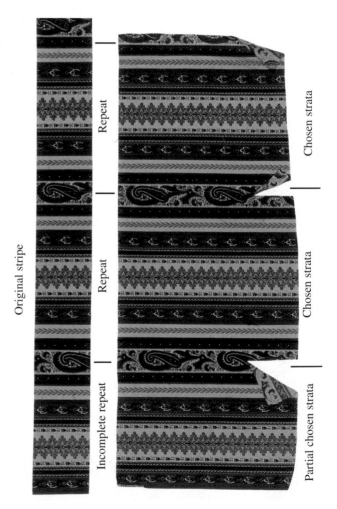

Decoding the fabric and preparing the stripe are important steps in mandala-making. In order to do these, you will need to mark the repeats of strata with pins. Note the number of repeats across the full fabric width. Decide whether this strata is the best use of fabric. Now, notch and then strip out (or trim out) the strata with scissors, carefully trimming down the center of each dividing stripe. Here, the motif mirrors out from the "lace" stripe; the lace stripe was a pivot point in the quilt Friendship Knot, page 100.

After a design layout is selected, the wedges are cut. Notice in every cutting that "waste" occurs. Waste is the spare parts of fabric between the wedge cuts. Waste occurs at the beginning and end of each strip of strata used. It also occurs between each wedge cut. Depending on the layout, these spare parts can produce a second entire mandala with an inverted design emphasis. This bonus mandala is often dramatically different from the original. In this book, bonus mandalas are labeled as "sister" quilts. South cuts can also be used as fan-shaped, corner-filling wedge borders, decorative spikes, and edge extensions.

The wedge positions in the design layout are identically duplicated across stripes and motifs in either single or multiple layers of strata. Wedge cuts in multiple layers of strata produce pairs of cuts or "partners." Partners can be either mirror images (layers right sides facing), or all one direction (both layers same side up). Partnered cuts, especially mirrored pairs, are usually sewn together. Keeping partners matched eliminates confusion of left and right cuts.

Organizing partnered cuts as each pair is cut, by piling crisscrossed, helps determine how many pairs have been cut. Crisscross piling, or collating, also helps determine how many more cuts are required to complete the mandala and it aids construction in the sewing phase. Collated partners can swiftly and consistently be fed the South end first through the sewing machine. Pairs (usually 20 or 12) are sewn in one long "kite-string" seam. In the kite string, the narrow South end of partnered wedges butts the wide North tip of the previously sewn partners.

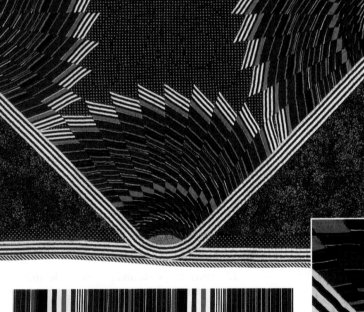

Fiesta. Approx. 54" x 54". Kelly green/red/navy on navy. 45-degree Sawtooth layout. It was laid out as quarter round units and has wedge-rounded corners on striped borders. Its "sister" quilt is Frantic (see page 46). Designed, pieced, and quilted by Sheila Finklestein.

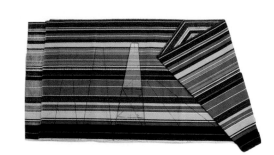

The Petal layout's positions are marked on this fabric in pen. Here the 15-degree ruler is used (with applied markings in red permanent marker).

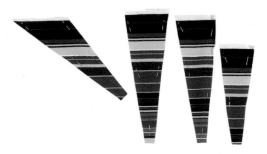

The Petal layout; 24 wedges are used to create the Petal layout (four sets of six). Pieces C, A, B, and D.

The Petal layout in sequence; place stacks next to the sewing machine in order! Pieces C mirror, B mirror, A, B, C, and D.

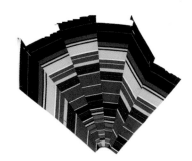

A completed petal (a quarter circle).

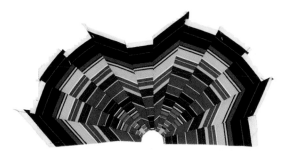

Two sewn petals (a half circle).

The completed circle with all four petals in place.

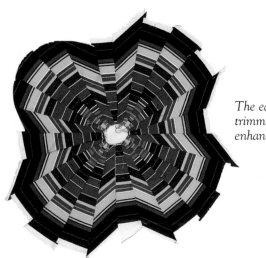

The edges have been trimmed on this petal to enhance its shape.

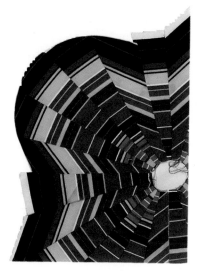

It is important that the seam allowance be exactly 1/4 inch, not a hair's width more or less. Any variance in one wedge will be multiplied 24 or 40 times! A hair off can cause a number of problems; for instance, it can cause the wedges to be too narrow to complete the full round or to be too wide. If seam allowances are smaller than 1/4 inch, the mandala will be more than 360 degrees and it will either widen the doughnut hole or distort the circle. If seam allowances are larger than 1/4 inch, the mandala will be less than 360 degrees and will not be large enough or connect and lie flat. In addition, if the seam allowance varies along the seam's length, it can cause ripples or volcano-like bulges across a sewn mandala's surface. A raised ridge-type seam guide that attaches to your sewing machine (magnetic or screw on) is recommended to insure precise consistent seaming. (Note: Magnetic guides are not recommended for computerized sewing machines.)

Careful pressing is needed to prevent distortion. Wedge cuts have bias edges that stretch easily. Sewn wedges, unlike other types of piecework, should not be pressed at every seam. Pressing should be done with a dry iron and should only be done after wedges are joined into quarter and half round units.

All seams should be pressed to the same side. Pressing should be done on the wrong side first, then repeated on the right side. Pressing on the right side flattens the surface and unfolds any tucks that occurred at the seam lines. When pressing, the key is to control stretching. Do not allow the rounded end of the ironing board to protrude through the donut hole (like a skirt). Support as much area as possible across the ironing board and limit the time loose areas are allowed to dangle over the ironing board's edge.

Steam pressing is reserved for finishing the full round mandala doughnut. The doughnut is steam pressed to prepare for the addition of the center and for the mandala to be mounted to the background.

WHAT IF my mandala has loops of fullness around the doughnut hole like ripples in a pond?

Two separate things may case "ripples" on a mandala: uneven seam depths or the mismatching of the South end of the wedge cuts.

Uneven seams can be corrected by using a seam guide to ensure straight, even seams, then ripping out only the seam wobble that protrudes past the new straightened seam. Try this correction on 8 (or 6) seams evenly spaced around your mandala. Re-press and check to see if this is enough or if additional seams must be reworked.

Mismatching of the South end of the wedge when sewing is a common error often used as a "quick fix" on wedges where the stripe is slightly off. Don't do it! Sliding those wedges causes ripples because the point-to-point matching of circumferences is disturbed (i.e. 3-inch circle circumference is being matched to the 3-1/2-inch circumference on an adjoining circle). The thick and thin of side-by-side wedges causes the bulges. To correct this, see how many wedges protrude into the doughnut hole. Mark the distance they protrude. Remove the wedges. Using this mark, position the South end of the wedge ruler at the mark. Trim the wedge and repeat as necessary. Re-sew wedges, matching South ends. Press and check to see that the mandala is pancake flat.

WHAT IF after I've ironed my mandala, it doesn't lie flat?

Several things can cause a mandala to not be pancake flat. The most common is too much pressing of seams and/or pressing with steam. Overpressing stretches the mandala's many bias grain lines and bias seams. Spread the mandala on a large surface (as flat as you can get). Hopefully it is evenly stretched in all directions. If not, check to see where the mandala is most badly stretched. Usually this occurs near the doughnut hole or near the perimeter.

It will be necessary to adjust the seams in the stretched area. Seam adjustment should be done in several evenly-spaced seams (the eighth or sixth). Adjusted seams will be the widest in the stretched area and taper down to nothing where the mandala appears flat. Make the same adjustment to each of the evenly-spaced seams. Check to see if the mandala is now flat. Will several more seams be required to get the mandala flat?

TIP VARIATIONS—
THE EDGES
OF THE MANDALA

Wedge tools were designed to create smooth, round medallions, but there are other possibilities available to enhance the edges of the mandala option you've chosen. The perimeter of the mandala can be decided at the cutting stage, or after the fact. Often, cutting errors provide delightful design input! Some options for edges include edge-stitched appliqué edges, some are faced, some are turned with purchased lace or trim, while others are sharply arrowed at the time they are stitched to their neighbors.

EXACT TRIM

An exact trimmed edge occurs when the wedges are cut. The wedge is cut on all four sides and produces a wedge, that when connected to several other wedges, produces a broad, even curve. Exact trim occurs when the wedge ruler, in the desired position, falls completely within the strata/stripe without overhanging the fabric. Fabric is rotary-cut away from the ruler on all four sides. This edge may simply be rolled to the underside of the medallion with your iron to be used as is, or as an interim step while trying to determine the overall design effect of your medallion.

WHAT IF the final wedge cut is too short or crooked by a corner that has been chopped off?

Two options can correct the problem: 1. Ignore the whole thing and use that shortened wedge as a design variation. Shorten all wedges that occur in that position in each repeated set. 2. Add on a piece of stripe or a coordinating color fabric to fill out the portion that was missing.

Fractures to Facets' irregular perimeter.

OVER-SHOOT THE NORTH

This jagged edge also occurs when the wedges are cut. It occurs when the North end of the ruler over-hangs the North edge of the strata/stripe. The wedge is cut on only three sides with the overhanging North edge left as is. It is a choppy edge, but it is dramatic and highlights the visual movement within the mandala design. Jagged edges are more challenging to roll to the underside. The Sawtooth edge requires a mitered fold at each wedge tip, but the dramatic results are worth the effort. The over-shoot cut may occur as a convenience. It can be treated as an interim step to be changed or to be retained at a later stage.

Over-shoot the North occurs when the North edge of the ruler extends beyond the strata, producing a wedge cut with an angled tip (shown at left).

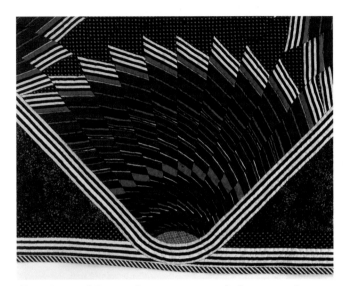

Fiesta's jagged Sawtooth perimeter is made from over-shoot wedges.

An over-shoot wedge from the 45-degree Sawtooth layout.

Roll hem

This is an over-shoot wedge. To be used as is, it must have each tip miter folded back. Pin and iron it back. Now, roll the remaining edge with an iron. Leave the pins in the tips until just before the machine catches them with a blind stitch.

CUTBACKS IN THE NORTH

Sometimes, it is necessary to trim back the North edge of any previously cut wedge. Reasons may include: the original cut was too long, the original cut was saw-toothed and that tooth is unattractive, or the doughnut is too large. The original cut must be accurate and carefully trimmed at the South. The narrow South end will become the reference point for skimming off the undesired top.

The wedge can be trimmed to any length. First, decide the length, then carefully shift the ruler to expose a seam allowance. Pencil dot the desired measurement in both the right and left side seam allowances. Slide the ruler down so that the North edge falls over and between the pencil dots. Check that the South edge of the wedge ruler falls even with (or parallel to) one of the horizontal measurement markings of the ruler (if it does not, go back and review your pencil dots). Pile several wedges and rotary-trim the North edge. Be sure to compare a wedge cut from each multi-cut pile to the first pile cut to check your accuracy—it is easier to make corrections now than later.

The original wedge end. The South end of ruler is aligned to a horizontal mark on the ruler.

Cutback in the North occurs when the angled tip of an over-shoot is not the desired tip.
To produce a straight ruler corrected tip, align the horizontal ruler marking with the previously cut South tip of the wedge. Trim off the angled North tip even with the ruler.

Here, the tip is being removed from an over-shoot wedge.

FANCY FINISHES FOR TIPS

SPIKES AND ARROWS

These are sharp angular points. They are made prior to seaming wedges into pairs (spikes) or at the time of sewing into pairs (arrows). These tips form their own faced edge and are stable and easy to appliqué to the background fabric.

INDIVIDUAL SPIKES

These are narrow angular points formed on a single wedge. Each "exact trim" or "cutback" wedge is folded carefully along its length, matching edges and North corners a 1/4 inch seam across the North edge of each folded wedge. (Note: This will not work on wedge cuts that "over-shoot" the North). Flip the sewn seam to the inside and match it up to the center fold line. Add one straight pin to anchor. Use a dull pencil or knitting needle to sharply turn the tip. Dry iron to crease. Repeat on all 40 (or 24) spike tips.

The reverse side of spikes with sewn tips.

Neon Nightmare's single wedge mitered tips.

ARROW OR PAIR POINTS

These are the double wedge versions of the above process. They are the fastest and most stable to create and to appliqué of all of the tip variations. Pair points are often used when mirror image wedges have been cut in a chevron layout. The resulting large arrow point further highlights the angular effect of the mirrored wedges.

Two "exact trim" or "cutback" wedges are seamed to

their neighbors with right sides together. But before opening to press, seam again across the North tips. Flip the seams to the inside, match the doubled wedge side seam to top seam, and pin. Use a dull pencil to push the seam's bulk out into a sharp arrow point. Dry iron each pair point. Note: The arrowed angle of your striped fabric will not always automatically fall even with the folded edge of your pair points. In most instances this is barely noticeable, while in others it tends to highlight the use of angles.

To complete a spike, turn and push out the tips with a pencil.
Match the A/B seam to the center of each single wedge and pin to prevent a shift of the angle. Seam "S" to "N" to another wedge. Note: On ovals, do not pin the angle in place until after seaming in order. Tips will be shifted according to the length needed to connect them.

Arrows begin with a pair of wedges. First, seam "S" to "N" into a pair. Then seam again to its partner across "N" tips. Note: This works only on straight or "cutback" tips.

B
A

Spikes and arrows are sharp, angular pointed tips that occur at the circumference. Here is a single wedge used in the Split Tip layout.

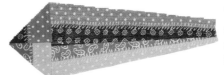

Turn and push out the tip with a pencil and match the seams up.

A/B
A/B

Spikes begin with single wedges. Match A to B, stitch from A/B to fold at center, and flash-feed through all of the wedges to be spiked.

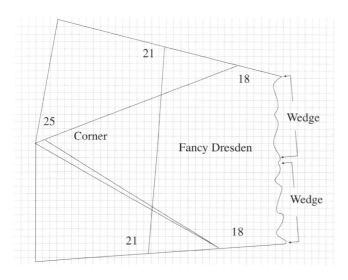

This angle is steeper than a sewn arrow... an extra long pair or arrow point tip.

Road to Candyland's double-wedge mitered tips.

The long spoke of the 9-degree Dresden. The single wedge shows the placement of the partial rose. The pointed tip is sharper here than a normal double wedge with a mitered tip. The seam is angled through the rose. The straight grain at the outer edge of the wedge "rescales" the rose.

CRULLERS

Crullers are a curvy variety of French doughnut. This term is also used to define a variety of scallops and shaped edges around a doughnut-shaped mandala. These curves are used to highlight a floral stripe or emphasize a petal shape. Curves can also be used to connect uneven lengths of measured wedges such as ovals or Dresden Plate variations.

Several methods can be used to create smooth curves. The paper pattern method uses dressmaker's pattern paper cut into the desired shape. Duplicate patterns are also cut. Then each pattern is straight-pinned in place on the fabric, lining up centers and seam lines. Machine stitching along the paper's curve stabilizes the bias and provides an accurate line for clipping and for pressing back the new curved edge.

Using freezer paper instead of dressmaker's pattern paper eliminates the need for pins. With the dull side up when ironed to the wrong side of fabric, freezer paper temporarily adheres to each wedge. This gives a stable edge to stay stitch and press to shape.

Floral Fan's scalloped tips.

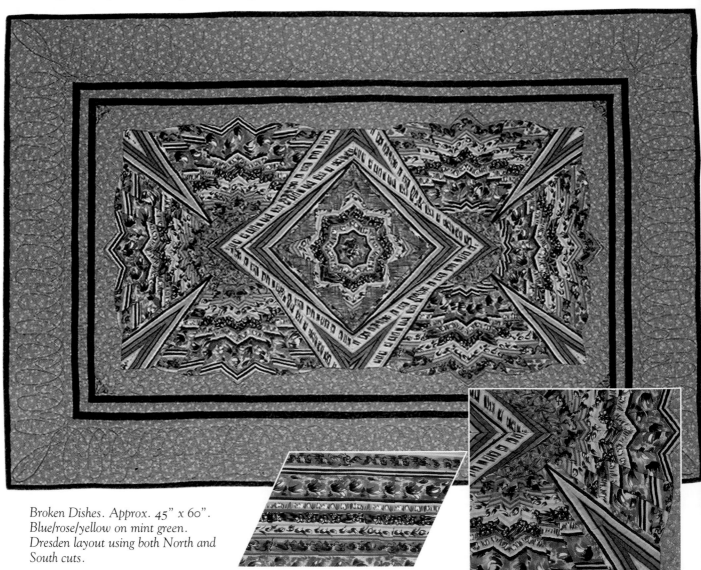

Broken Dishes. Approx. 45" x 60".
Blue/rose/yellow on mint green.
Dresden layout using both North and
South cuts.

Facing the edge (like that on a dress neckline) is a more lengthy process, but it makes a stable, uniform curve or arch. These curves can then be easily machine appliquéd or left loose as a dimensional "petal" edge. The facing may either be a separate layer of fabric (like a neckline facing, Fig. A) or the extended North edge of a wedge folded back against itself (Fig. B, next page).

A patterned curve is then positioned, matching seams and centers. A machine-stitched seam replaces what was stay stitching in the previous method. Trimming and clipping of the stitched line, however, remain the same. The facing is rolled to the underside and pressed. Pressing often evens out any nicks or bumps in the stitched curve. The facing layer provides an extra layer of stability, a plus when adding appliqué curves to its background fabric.

Several different tools are useful for drafting curves. One is a dressmaker's ruler (French curve), which is an "S"-shaped ruler. The other is a flexible curve (drafting "snake"), which offers the option of creating a curve of your own design. This curve is a multi-jointed drafting tool that allows you to create or duplicate a variety of exotic shapes.

To create a curve, lay the multiple wedge unit on your rotary mat. Be sure at least one side lines up to its straight grid line for a reference point. Position the curve tool across the sewn multi-wedge unit (Fig. C, next page). Position it connecting all lengths without allowing dog-eared or V-ed cutouts at any of the seams. Following the curved tool, mark the wedge unit with a pencil or chalk. Mark the tool with pen or tape at the start and stop spots as well. This helps find the same spot (curve location) to use on additional wedge units. Remove the curve tool from the multi-wedge unit. View your curve. Is the curve smooth, without bumps or dents? Does it appear harmonious with the motif or floral within the wedge unit? Does the curve need to be evened, adjusted, or repositioned?

Fig. A

Facing the edge makes a stable, uniform curve or arch. A separate facing (either bias or straight grain) can be added to achieve this. Make the facing for the length of the wedge needed (here, folding it back would shorten it too far). Pencil in a curve, stitch, trim and clip the seam, and finally, turn and press.

Not Kansas Anymore's scalloped "petal edge" perimeter.

Curves tilt in both oval and Dresden mandalas (See Chapter 6, More Mandala Techniques). Mirrored cuts are created to give both a right- and left-handed tilt. They are created by piling two identical wedge units right sides together. Both units are then cut as one piece. When pulled apart, the curves will be the mirror reversed tilt of each other. Curves can be pencil-marked and scissor-trimmed, but it is faster to pile and rotary-trim several curved units at once. Wedge units are layered, the French curve is positioned, and the rotary cutter trims around it, making several identical curve cuts at once. The flexible design curve can also be used to rotary cut, but the pressure exerted with your cutter can distort your chosen design curve. Making paper patterns or templates of the flexible curve eliminate this problem.

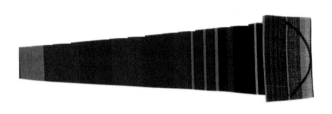

Fig. B

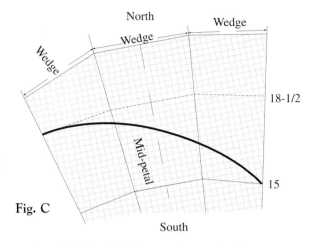

Fig. C

For cruller-curved tips, the North tip of the wedge is folded back against the wedge (note that the "N" cut is wider than wedge when in position). The curve to be used is penciled in position, and a seam is stitched over the design line. Trim back the seam to 1/8 inch, clip the curves, and turn and press the curves. Finally add it to the next wedge.

For right and left-handed tilts, two layers of wedge units are piled right-sides together and trimmed as one unit.

TRIMS

Trims are yet another way to roll back the edge of the medallion and provide a clean, even, finished edge for appliqué or edge stitch. Commercially available bias tape, piping (regular and jumbo), gathered lace, ruffled eyelet, and rickrack are all possibilities. The important thing to remember when considering a trim for this purpose is, does it bend? Does it have the flexibility to curve without straining, pulling, or popping up on the furthest curve? All trims should be preshrunk. If the trim binds or shrinks, it acts as a drawstring, distorting areas both within and beyond the doughnut. Trims are usually applied while the medallion is still separate from its background, or instead of a background, such as the bias edges on War Bonnet or the jumbo piping on Ripples.

When deleting a background, the doughnut edge should be stay stitched at 1/4 inch in from the cut edge. Stay stitching provides insurance against the stretching caused by persuading a trim into position. Note: When trimming as the final edge finish, stay stitch through all layers. Then add the step of a triple

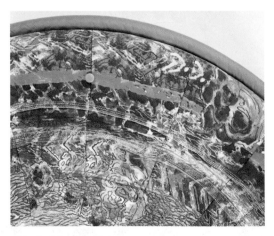

Ripples' jumbo piping.

zigzag or serpentine stitch over the raw edge to provided the most firm, even surface to bind.

Lace or rickrack, added to the mandala edge, are stitched into place when stay stitching the edge, the stitching placed at whatever measurement is convenient to use with your trim. On many lace trims it is ideal to stitch at the connecting seam line of your lace to its bias, but not every trim is made with this feature. Often lining the tips of the rickrack with the raw edge of the mandala and eyeballing a seam line right down its center is the method for stitching. Use your iron to gently flip the stay stitched trim and the raw edge to the underside of the medallion.

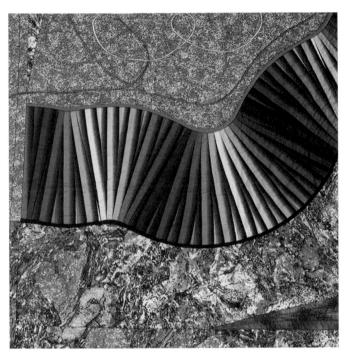

Rocky Road's bias perimeter.

Raw edges   Raw edges

Iron

Raw edges

Blind stitch

Bias tape trim. Wedge units are anchored to the background with edge stitching or fusibles. The mandala's raw edges are still visible. Use a double-folded bias and stitch the bias to the mandala through all thicknesses. Press and roll the bias to cover the raw edges (with an iron). Blind stitch the bias folded edge to the background, covering the raw edge.

Double
bias
tape

Stay stitched edge

Trims are applied to the mandala's stay stitched edge, usually before attaching it to the background. They are applied to the edge with a straight stitch at a convenient seam (in the edge of the bias on the ruffle or base of a design or lace).

Seam allowance and trim truned to

Stay stitching

For rickrack, align the tips with the mandala edge, then eyeball the seam right through the rickrack's center.

The finished edge is then straight stitched in the ditch (as shown here) or blind stitched to the background.

Occasionally, to simplify construction, a bias edging will be applied after the medallion or its parts are attached to the background. The wedge units are anchored either by edge stitching or adhesive (fusible) to the background. Doubled bias tape is positioned atop the units, matching raw edges. Stitch through all layers of anchoring tape, wedges, and the background as one. Using an iron, slide the iron toward the raw edge, flipping the tape to the outside and concealing the raw edges. Machine edgestitch or blind stitch the bias tape fold to the background.

TIP EXTENSIONS

Tip extensions are additions to previously cut single wedges or multiple wedge sections. They add visual focus and are a clarification to your original layout. They add distance where it was originally unavailable or unanticipated. Tip extensions fill in, finish a point, or extend an arc. They can be used in any design layout but appear most often in Pinwheel and Dresden layouts.

Tip extensions are often scavenged from the secondary South cuts or the "spare parts" that occur at the beginning and end of each length of strata used. The size and availability of the spare parts determine the length and number of extensions that can be cut. Strata with large motifs may have spare parts with very little motif remaining. The motif available may not be in a location usable for matching to the existing mandala.

Playing with the spare parts is the only way to see if they can fill out the design. This "play" is called "auditioning," where strata pieces are physically slid into position to see if they "fit the part." Corners and raw edges are tipped and manipulated until a stripe is capped or mitered, or a motif is matched.

Normal piecing of multiple-angled extensions to a mandala is difficult. An easy method of adding extensions is by "faking" the seams with a machine blind stitch and monofilament thread. Extensions created by auditioning are folded and straight pinned into position. Then a tiny blind stitch anchors each fold down. Extra bulk is trimmed from seams and overlapping layers.

Note: In Friendship Knot, the tip extensions, the lace edges, became the design emphasis. Each "lace" tip extension in that design was cut from a single narrow stripe (see Rings and Frames, page 100). An extension was sewn to each wedge before it was sewn to adjoining wedges.

Friendship Knot's pieced Bullseye perimeter.

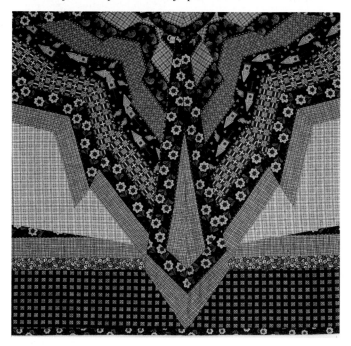

Double Dish's tip extension spokes.

DOUGHNUT HOLES:

THE CENTER OF THE MANDALA

Your eye is drawn to the center of a mandala design. Filling the doughnut hole focuses and completes the design. The artistic choices you make can either enhance the swirling visual movement or pull the plug on an otherwise good design. The options for filling the hole may be as simple as a fabric circle or as complex as a mariner's compass. It can take several attempts to find the perfect design fit. There have been occasions when a mandala resists numerous centers. Don't rush into a mediocre decision. Enlist a trusted quilting friend's advice, or use an instant camera photo of your options.

Oriental Mandala. 60-degree Chevron layout. The flowered stripe was an inexpensive piece of fabric that turned out to be a beautiful mandala with an Oriental touch. Silk ribbon flowers were added to the center to complete the look. Designed, machine pieced, and quilted by Sue Gerbick.

Begin by accurately measuring the opening. To get an accurate measurement, firmly press your mandala with an iron. This is the time when you want to use steam. It is usually best to press seams all to the same side so the seams spiral one way completely around the medallion. This eliminates the distortion that can be caused by thick piles of overlapping seams. Then measure across the center in several directions. It is important that the center fabric be larger than the opening. Use the longest measurement plus 1 inch to determine the size of the doughnut hole. An embroidery hoop in a size close to the donut hole measurement makes a great "window" for auditioning possible centers.

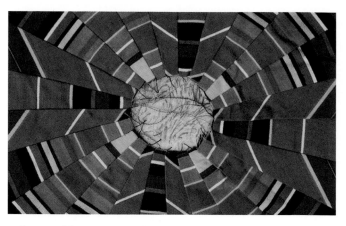

The mandala is on its background, but the doughnut hole is not yet filled.

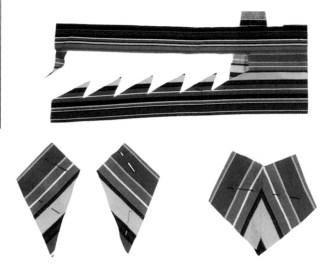

Shown are the fabric leftovers from previous wedge cuts, a mirrored pair (layers face together), and the mirrored pair sewn together. Four sets of mirrored pairs will make up an eight-patch center.

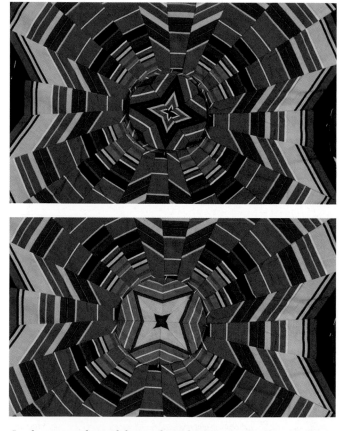

Look at several possibilities when plugging the doughnut hole.

The eight-patch center is put together; here you can see its seams. Note how the eight pieces are trimmed down to a circle.

Here the eight-patch center is pinned in place.

The pre-plugged doughnut hole.

The doughnut hole is filled with a four-patch center.

The simplest of centers are a single circle of fabric, often made of background fabric or a fabric of coordinating color. These centers create a visual void—the design illusion of actually seeing through the doughnut and beyond into space. Simple circles can be made from a coordinating large-scale print. Sometimes the stripe itself includes an extra-large motif that can be plugged into the center of the mandala. Some stripes have coordinated pre-printed "cheater" quilt blocks. These cheater blocks make deceptively intricate plugs.

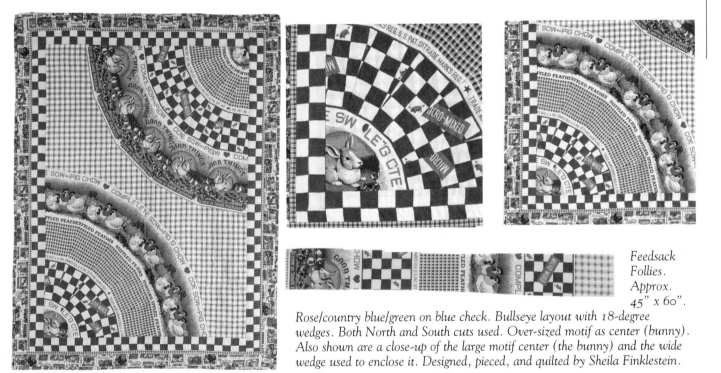

Feedsack Follies. Approx. 45" x 60".

Rose/country blue/green on blue check. Bullseye layout with 18-degree wedges. Both North and South cuts used. Over-sized motif as center (bunny). Also shown are a close-up of the large motif center (the bunny) and the wide wedge used to enclose it. Designed, pieced, and quilted by Sheila Finklestein.

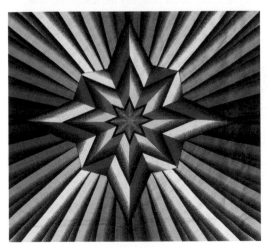

Portal's cheater panel center.

Sunflower's cheater panel center.

The background was trimmed away and the center needle-darned in place.

Several repeats of the motif may be pulled together to create a kaleidoscope version of the original. This circle is constructed as a four-square. Each square can contain a whole or partial segment of the motif.

Pink Ribbons and Roses; four-patch center rose.

Scarab's four-patch center.

Medicine Wheel's four-patch center.

Floral Fan's four-patch center.

A four-patch center is a circle cut from four squares that are seamed together.

A five-section division of a circle works well for 9-degree mandalas. Each section seam intersects every eighth seam of a 40-wedge mandala. Seam matching gives a sense of continuity. Seam matching also aids accurate placement of the center. A five-section center can be finished as a circle, a five-point star, or a pentagon.

A six-section center is ideal for 15-degree mandalas. Every seam of the center intersects the 24-wedge mandala at every fourth seam. A six-section center can be finished as a hexagon, a circle, or a star. A variety of commercial templates are available to make 60-degree triangles to cut this center.

Wheel of Fortune's five-patch center.

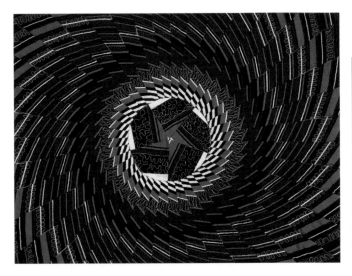

Frantic's five-patch center.

Fractures to Facets' five-patch center.

Tilting at Pinwheel's five-patch center.

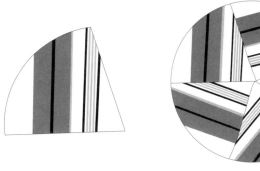

A single patch and the five-patch center it is a part of.

Eight-section centers also work well for either 9- or 15-degree wedge mandalas. Each of the eight seams evenly intersects the mandala at every fifth (or third) seam. Eight-section centers can be finished as a circle, an octagon (with straight sides), or star points that overlay both the doughnut hole and the mandala. These octagons can be squeezed out of the smallest slivers of spare parts or combined with coordinating fabrics.

Sundance's eight-patch center.

Double Dish's eight-patch center.

Miracle Grown's eight-patch center.

Tribal Shield's eight-patch center.

*Note the original stripe and
the variety of centers that can
be derived from it.*

*Eight-patch centers. Note the position
of the stripe on a one-eighth section to
form a star or octagon.*

Applying the plug you've chosen to fill the doughnut hole is easy once the design decisions are made. The edges of most plugs are bias. To assure flat, even circles, cut a freezer paper circle to the needed measurement (a dime-store compass makes small circles a breeze). Iron the freezer paper to the marked circle to stabilize all of the bias grains (the paper provides firm edges to iron) or glue stick the raw edges over.

Or, instead of freezer paper, mark the required measurement with a compass on the wrong side of the fabric circle, then machine stay stitch along that mark. The upper machine tension should be slightly tighter than normal. This increased tension helps the edge to curl to the wrong side. Press to the underside just a hair beyond the stay stitching, but do not trim yet. Check the plug over the mandala. Is the design what you expected or do you need to explore further? After you have found the perfect center, trim the raw edge to 1/4 inch. Plug the center, matching seams and motifs if necessary. Straight-pin the plug in place. Pins should be no farther than 1/2 inch apart.

Tools used to cut centers (a circle template and a compass).

Centers can be appliquéd with a machine blind stitch or edge-stitched with a straight stitch. Hand appliqué is another possibility, but the multitude of seam bulk may pose a challenge. An especially ragged edge motif can be fused in place, then lightly machine needle darned into position.

THE BACKGROUND

Once your mandala is sewn, it is ready for a background or the option of finishing it as a round quilt. This requires either a dig through your fabric stash or a field trip to the fabric store (it is important that the mandala go along with you). To prevent stretching damage, the mandala should be prepared for the trip. Cut a piece of paper, muslin, or fleece slightly smaller than the diameter of the mandala. Secure the mandala to the paper with straight pins. Pin every few inches along wedge seams. This anchors the mandala to another mostly straight grain unit to allow many foldings, unfoldings, and holding up for admiring onlookers!

Walk past the shelves with the mandala opened pie-shaped. Allow the center and a dominant motif to hang out. As you pass, notice what fabrics make the mandala sparkle. Pull out several options, both prints and solids. Be open-minded! Make a pile of fabric bolts.

Auditioning different background fabrics can be both fun and challenging.

Find an empty counter or stretch of floor. Unwind a piece of each fabric bolt longer than the diameter of your mandala. Using two similar prints, lay both lengths of fabric fold-to-fold on the floor. Open the mandala. Center it over the fabric options. Review the choices. Step back as far from the auditioning area as you can get and still see both fabrics equally. Generally the field of options narrows quickly. One or two fabric options will appear to brighten, focus, or even make it glow. Go for the most intense or the most appealing.

Notice how much fabric is extending beyond the mandala. Is this mandala an open-ended design exercise or are there size limitations? Consider the wall space or bed size the mandala is intended for (see page 19). Approximate that size in the chosen fabric. That increase or decrease in background area may effect your perception of the background fabric. The background may seem to overwhelm or swallow-up the mandala, or the background may seem to dissolve or no longer be strong enough to support the mandala. Look for a balance between the design focus, the mandala, and the background.

Sometimes indecision or time stops us in our tracks. At this point either buy a single yard of the "almost all right" fabric as a sample or plan to start the fabric quest again later. Label your sample with the store name, phone number, and reference numbers. If after continued quests, it still is "almost right" you can call to hold or credit card purchase knowing that you've explored all of this season's options.

Calculate the required yardage. Often a bed-sized quilt requires two lengths of standard 45-inch wide to completely cover the space. A mandala quilt usually has only one central seam. Compare whether it is most economical for the seam to fall horizontal or vertical.

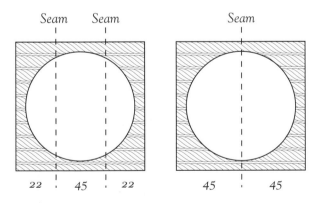

For example, the needed size is 60 x 75 inches.

For the quilt to have one vertical seam, it will take two lengths of 75 inches each. The background after sewing will be 90 inches (45 x 2) and 75 inches long. It will require 4-1/2 yards of fabric.

For the quilt to have one horizontal seam, it will take two lengths of 60 inches each. The background after sewing will be 60 inches wide and 90 inches long. It will take 120 inches (3-3/4 yards) of fabric.

Always allow extra yardage for straightening lengths of fabric!

When choosing background fabrics, don't be afraid to audition several different colors and patterns.

These two looked the best…

And the winner is… This fabric really helps bring out the blue accents in the medallion.

Finishing Mandalas Without a Background

Some mandala medallions are completed without a background mounting fabric. These mandalas are round quilted pieces with finished edges. The edges can be finished in several ways, including binding, piping, or facing the entire edge. Sometimes a hanging sleeve or other mechanism is included in that edge finish to allow the mandala to hang evenly.

A hanging sleeve for a circular quilt is an additional flap of fabric that spans the back of the quilt. The flap is usually one-third to one-half of the mandala's circumference, is half-moon shaped, and extends from edge to edge. The curved side is included in the bound or piped edge finish and the flat side is hemmed, but not attached to the quilt back. This creates a large pocket between the quilt back and the flap of the hanging sleeve. Some kind of stiffener is added in this pocket to support the curved top of the mandala. The stiffener can be cardboard, buckram, plywood, or foamcore board. The stiffener is cut to the actual finished size of the pocket. The fit should be snug. Do not make an allowance for the depth of the wood or foamcore board. The quilt and pocket will stretch slightly to allow the stiffener to be eased into place. A loop of narrow ribbon or a metal or plastic curtain ring is sewn to the hanging sleeve at the center top of the mandala for wall mounting.

Another option for supporting the curved edge of the mandala is a hoop. Hoops come in a number of sizes for embroidery and quilting purposes, but many finished mandalas are larger than a standard quilting hoop. A large, light-weight alternative to a quilting hoop is a child's hula-hoop. Hula-hoops come in 27- and 36-inch diameters. They can be cut down from their original size or several hoops can be spliced

Ripples. Bullseye layout in a "marginal stripe" (here, the stripe itself is secondary to the rose motif). It has a lot of surface embellishment with machine techniques and hand-sewn beads that were supposed to emphasize the bubbles and ripples created when a pebble is dropped in a pond. The quilt is finished with jumbo piping. Designed, pieced, and quilted by Sheila Finklestein.

together to form a bigger circle.

Using a hoop to support a mandala's curved edge also requires a pocket of fabric. The pocket surrounds the entire circumference of mandala and is made of purchased bias binding or bias cut strips. The binding is an extra-wide size, which is included in the piping or bound edge finish. It is doubled in half lengthwise, forming a tunnel to insert a drawstring. The drawstring can be made of grosgrain ribbon or twill tape. When the drawstring is pulled tightly it forms a narrow pocket around the circumference of the mandala. The hoop is inserted in that narrow pocket and the string is tightly knotted. The pocket edge can be left as is or secured to the quilt's back with safety pins or hand stitching.

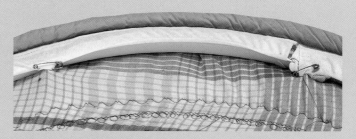

A full view of Ripples' plaid-back with its hula-hoop mounting.

A close-up of the tunnel where the drawstring is inserted. When the drawstring is pulled tightly it forms a narrow pocket around the circumference of the mandala. Note the hoop tucked under the drawstring tunnel and the safety pins that prevent the hoop from popping out of the formed pocket.

Here you can see the underside's seam.

MOUNTING THE DOUGHNUT BACKGROUND

There is more to mounting the doughnut than slapping the circle down and gluing it in place. A few simple tricks ensure this process goes smoothly.

The background, or mounting fabric, can be either a pieced or solid unit. For speed and ease of manipulation, choose a single unit. Whichever you choose, though, it should be wider and longer than your medallion. A minimum of 3 inches on each side works very well, but scraping by on 1/2 inch on all sides can yield beautiful results. Always start with an area larger than you feel you will need. Margins can always be straightened or trimmed down later in the design process. Adding extra is more of a chore.

Begin by pressing the mounting fabric to remove wrinkles, then fold in half, and again into quarters. Folds should be lightly creased with the iron. Find an extra-large surface to work on (a pair of cafeteria

tables, a Ping-Pong table, or an open stretch of tiled or hardwood floor). Open the mounting fabric, right side facing you, and with masking tape, secure one edge of it to some straight mark on your surface (i.e. a length of floorboard). Go to the opposite side of the fabric and gently smooth, till taut. Do not stretch! Mounting fabric should appear absolutely flat but not distorted. Tape in place. Slight indents of the half and quarter press lines will still be noticeable. Repeat taping process on the remaining sides.

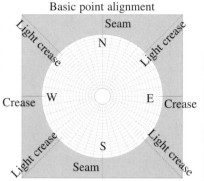

Basic point alignment

It is easiest to mount the doughnut on a single large square of fabric that is larger than the medallion (many medallions will be larger than most standard fabric widths). If you need to piece the background, it is easiest on two equal lengths of fabric where the mandala is placed over one central seam (unlike a backing where two seams balance the distance). After seaming, press and lightly crease at quarters and eighths. Align the quarter and eighth creases to every fifth seam of the mandala, pin, and smooth and pin between the markings.

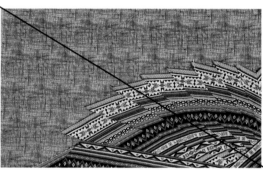

By creasing the background into quarters and eighths, you can center the mandala on its background with ease.

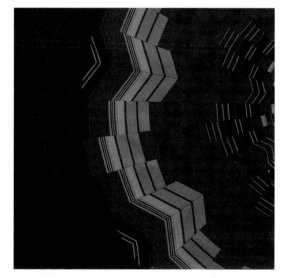

A close-up of a center medallion's top stitching.

Now the mandala's edge is pressed to the wrong side.

To prepare the mandala for mounting, pin mark it at every quarter (every tenth or sixth seam line). Align the pins with the creased half and quarter marks on the mounting fabric. Anchor with pins to the quarter marks. Gently pat the remaining areas of wedges down evenly between those points. The medallion should be pancake flat against the background (for tips, see page 57). With one hand placed atop the medallion to prevent shifting, straight pin the medallion to the mounting fabric at 1/2-inch intervals.

After the entire mandala has been securely pinned down, release the masking tape on all edges. With the tape released, check for any shifting, bubbles, or puckers in either the mandala or its background (caused by over stretching the mounting fabric during taping). Repeat as needed. When you've achieved a pinned pancake-flat mount, the edge of the mandala may be edge-stitched or appliquéd in place. The machine blind stitch with nylon monofilament is a favored method of appliqué. The length of the ditch stitches should equal less than 1/2 inch between horizontal picks into the mandala. Manually stalling the machine's forward movement at sharp pointed tips, make several horizontal picks at the same spot. This ensures the points are securely anchored down and will not curl up or pull loose.

On very wide medallions, two rectangles of fabric may be required to span the distance. Remove selvages and press edges. Unlike a quilt's back, rectangles are butted and sewn edge-to-edge in one central seam. A mandala will camouflage a greater area of that seam when centered. The tape and pin sequences remain the same during mounting. Occasionally you may want the seams to show, to act as further design elements to your medallion. Additionally, the seams themselves will be used as reference points when placing of intricate or multiple mandala designs.

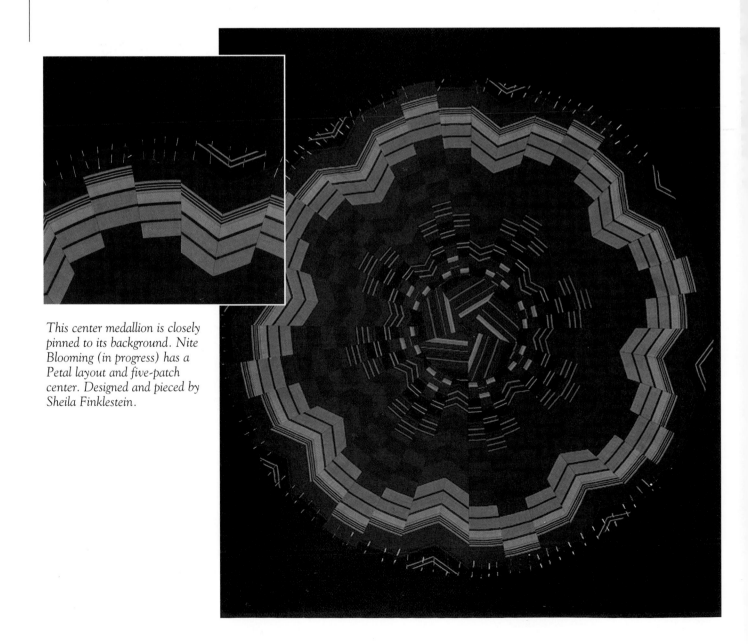

This center medallion is closely pinned to its background. Nite Blooming (in progress) has a Petal layout and five-patch center. Designed and pieced by Sheila Finklestein.

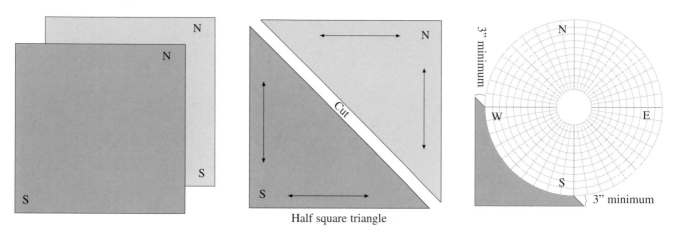

Half square triangle

When there is not enough background yardage, two half-square triangles can be substituted. Fold yardage into a perfect square, double thick. Test if the mandala half fits within a half square of the available yardage.

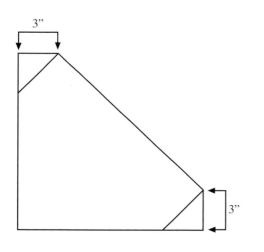

Fold back the tips at a 3-inch marking.

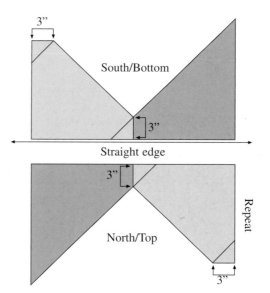

South/Bottom

Straight edge

North/Top

Repeat

On a cutting mat or other straight mark, line up the straight edge of two triangles and repeat. Pin and/or bast the 3-inch joints.

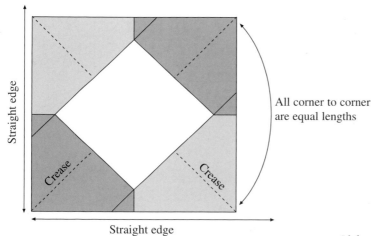

All corner to corner are equal lengths

Check for enough underlay for seams; readjust if needed. Match quarter and eighth points of the mandala to the seams and crease.

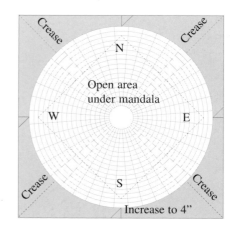

Open area under mandala

Increase to 4"

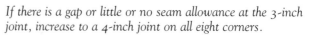

If there is a gap or little or no seam allowance at the 3-inch joint, increase to a 4-inch joint on all eight corners.

SEAM VARIATIONS FOR MANDALA BACKGROUNDS

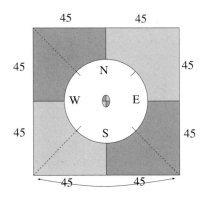

Approx. 90 background

You can piece available yardage or an added design element (for example, printed muslin with two different patterns or subtle color changes) to mount the doughnut on a four-square background. Seams can act as placement guides.

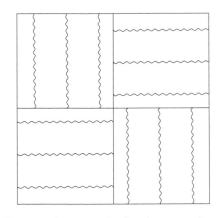

You can also create further design emphasis by manipulating a directional or striped background.

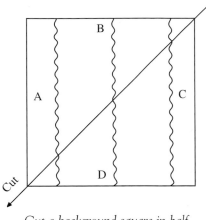

Cut a background square in half.

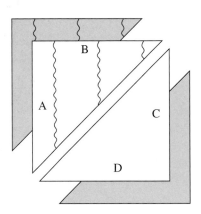

Pair two striped squares with right sides together (this equals four triangles).

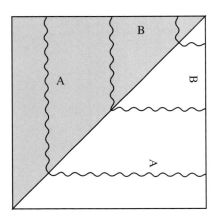

Open a pair and match up the bias seams.

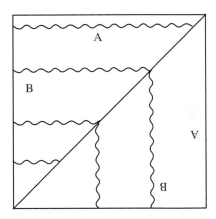

The Chevron seamed striped square. (Four partnered squares equals two triangles.)

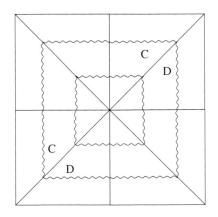

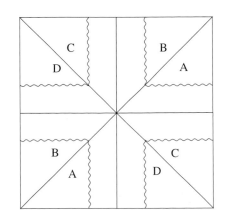

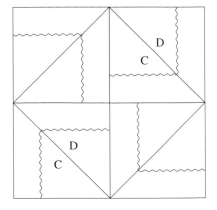

Possible configurations of Chevron backgrounds. All enhance the visual "spin" of a mandala.

LOST IN SPACE

Occasionally, after mounting the mandala to its background, it will appear to have "shrunk" visually or lost its focus. This often occurs when too much empty space surrounds the medallion. Sit back and evaluate how your mandala is developing. Consider a few questions to determine if you should trim off the excess, fill it in, or quilt in the void space.

What is the quilt's intended use? Was the background's size merely a convenience? Was it a standard fabric width or a size that occurred by doubling two fabric lengths? Test for possible down-sizing by laying the quilt on a large surface. Fold several inches on each side to the back, out of view. Does shrinking the background help the quilt appear more focused? Have you reserved enough striped fabric for borders? If so, those "lost" inches can be "made up" with an addi-tional border. What is the maximum distance the reserved stripe will surround? Is that distance shorter than the distance around the current background space? Must the background be folded back even further to fit the reserved borders? Will you fold back evenly on all sides or will it become more rectangular?

Still a toss-up? Examine your leftover fabrics. They can be used here to fill in the voids at the corners and add further design emphasis (see Wedge-Angled and Wedge-Curved Borders, pages 85 and 89, respectively). Depending on what remains, corners can be filled a number of ways. Fan shapes, appliquéd decorative spikes, or directional markers are just three. Leftovers of odd angles can fill in corners, too. It is not necessary for all corners to be identical. An uneven fill of corners expands the visual spin of a mandala into the border space. Filling only two opposing corners can add an interesting directional touch by directing the eye along a skewed diagonal path.

Medicine Wheel's corners were filled with leftover parts.

Sunny's Day. Approx. 60" x 80". Pink/purple/yellow on pale lavender. 60-degree Sawtooth. Both North and South cuts were used (for the medallion and corner fill). Its "sister" quilt is Green Fantom (see page 49). This is a good example of "lost in space." Designed and pieced by Sheila Finklestein. Quilted by Helen Wiley.

TO TRIM OR NOT TO TRIM

After the mandala is firmly sewn to its background, if you are a machine quilter or intend to have your piece commercially quilted, you can stop here. If, however, you plan to hand quilt it, you need to remove the mounting fabric from behind the medallion.

To do this, lift your quilt off its flat surface, and hold it in your lap. Pinch the top surface of the mandala in one hand and the back of the background in the opposite hand. Gently pull the surfaces apart, creating a balloon of air between them. In an area under the mandala, nick the mounting fabric with scissors, being careful not to nick the mandala as you cut. Slide the fingers of your non-scissors hand between the mounting fabric you are removing and the mandala. Carefully remove the backing, allowing just a scant 1/4-inch seam allowance to remain.

Circle of Roses. 84" x 100". Mauve background with black and rose border print fabric. 60-degree Chevron layout. Large medallion in center and four smaller ones in each corner. The creator said she was "inspired by my sister, Lola Finnell, to take this mandala class from Sheila Finklestein. It was very interesting using border prints and the 9-degree wedge ruler." This quilt won third place in the "Gone to Pieces Quilt Club" quilt show (Pieced Quilt category) held in September 1997 in Ashland, KY. Pieced and quilted by Janice Riley.

BORDER BASICS

The purposes of a border are to stabilize the edge and to outline and highlight a quilt's design. Some basic border rules apply to all quilts—but they are often unknown or ignored. Improperly applied borders distort a quilt's surface, producing "dog-eared" stretched corners or edges that ruffle and twist.

Begin by measuring the quilt top across the quilt's center both vertically and horizontally. Do not measure along the edges. Do not assume that because you followed a "recipe" that your quilt came out with identical measurements to that recipe. The measurements on parallel edges may not be equal. In fact, when comparing the top, middle, and bottom, all three measurements may be different. Several things may have caused the variation, including inaccurate seams, stretching during pressing, over-handling, or presser foot or machine changes.

Borders cut from the lengthwise grain of fabric (parallel to woven edge) will have less stretch than those borders cut from the more economical width-wise fabric grain. In width-wise borders, the grain is also less likely to be even throughout. Also, cross-cut borders usually require seams to achieve adequate length for large quilts. Those seams should be bias if possible.

Consider the following in determining the length of borders: Are all corners perfectly squared? Do the side measurements vary from the center measurement? Is that amount larger than 3/8 inch? (A difference of 3/8 inch or less can be eased into place, but a larger variation will require trimming or restitching of seams at equal distances from each other across the quilt's surface.)

Both side borders should be cut to the "average" length, which will generally be the length across the center. Both the quilt's top and the side borders should be folded and lightly creased at the half and quarter points. Align and pin the quarter and half marks on the quilt to those on the border strips. Align and pin the beginning and the end edges to each other. With the border on top (a walking foot is helpful), stitch the borders to the quilt, easing where necessary. Again, check for square corners with a quilter' square or T-square. Repeat the measuring process on the center, top, and bottom edges. Notice that this round of border contains the addition of two times the depth of the border strip. Cut both the top and bottom borders the same measurement. Again, crease at quarter and half marks on quilt and the borders, align both, and stitch together. Parallel edges will be equal. Handling and pressing a quilt can cause stretching, so this method should be repeated for each set of borders added.

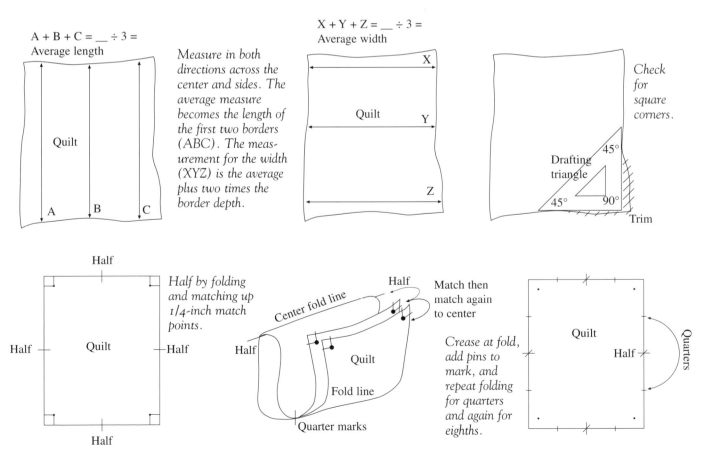

A + B + C = __ ÷ 3 =
Average length

Measure in both directions across the center and sides. The average measure becomes the length of the first two borders (ABC). The measurement for the width (XYZ) is the average plus two times the border depth.

X + Y + Z = __ ÷ 3 =
Average width

Check for square corners.

Drafting triangle 45° 45° 90°
Trim

Half by folding and matching up 1/4-inch match points.

Match then match again to center

Crease at fold, add pins to mark, and repeat folding for quarters and again for eighths.

For borders with mitered corners, the measurements of the quilt's center will be added to two times the depth of the border plus a 1/2 inch of seam on both the East and West and the North and South lengths. The creasing and alignment of mitered borders is similar to that of border with square corners, however, the end points, where stitching begins and stops, is different. On the quilt top, stitching begins and ends 1/4 inch within the top. On border strips the first stitch occurs at the miter seam line, which is one times the border's width, within the border strip on both ends. This leaves loose tails of border strip at the beginning and the end. Those loose tails are then folded back at a 45-degree angle. Check for accuracy with the bias line on your ruler or a 45/90-degree triangle. Crease with an iron, pin, then hand or machine stitch in place. Miters stretch ("dog-ear") easily. Double-check that the corners have remained an accurate 90-degree angle.

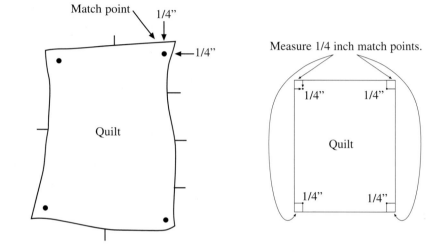

This is the folded back "dog ear." Match the point to a quarter-inch corner.

Begin at the match point and mark the average length for each corresponding border strip. Now quarter and eight each strip. Finally, match the border marking to the quilt marks, pin, and sew ease if necessary.

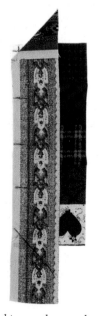

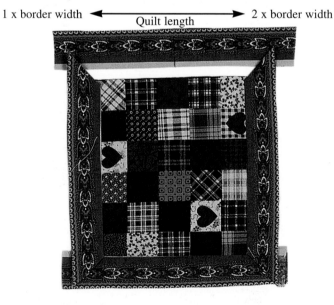

Begin stitching at the match point, but do not catch the tail.

Here, the final border strip and tails are loose. At this point, check for the pattern match and true bias at the corner with a 45-degree triangle. Pin the border tails in place and press. Hand or machine appliqué.

WEDGE-ANGLED BORDERS

These borders are wedge-shaped and cut with extra-long wedge rulers. Wedge-angled borders are a combination of both pieced and machine appliqué techniques. They vary the visual depth of field, the illusion that some parts of the background are deeper or further away than others. This illusion is created by a shift in color or pattern within the background. Varying the depth of field can be a pure design choice or an effort to expand limited yardage. (Standard width yardage is often too narrow to span the area beneath a large mandala without some pieced additions.) Wedge angle additions (rather than straight strip additions) add a subtle design element to what usually is void space. Wedge-angled borders are made by insertion, appliqué, or extension.

Wedge-angled borders can be achieved in several ways. The easiest is the inserting of a leftover (South) wedge. This wedge is inserted into a seam. This wedge can stand alone or as an addition to a linear border. The wedge is folded along its length, raw edges matched, and inserted into a seam. The folded insert can either be appliquéd or left loose to provide a three-dimensional accent.

An example of Rocky Road's wedge-angled borders. These were decorative overlays of the existing background.

Part of Portal's wedge-angled borders.

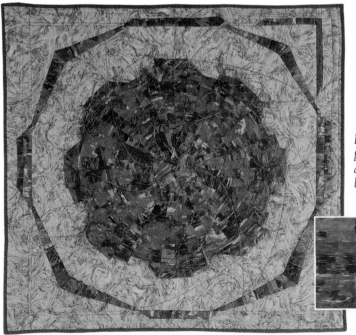

Fractures to Facets. Approx. 45" x 45". Mustard/teal/rose on pink. Five-position drop match layout. Spare parts were used as string borders. This quilt has a five-patch center. Its irregular perimeter was dictated by the length of the wedges cut.

Designed, pieced, and quilted by Sheila Finklestein. From the collection of Dr. Paul Iahn, Cleveland, OH.

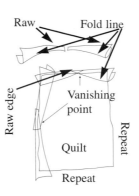

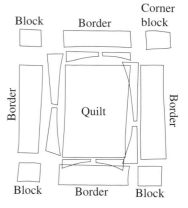

Pin and baste in position and trim the excess. Apply the borders as usual.

Baste the wedge to the border strip then match and sew to the quilt center.

Wheel of Fortune's wedge-angled borders (folded inserts).

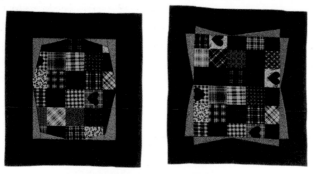

Decorative 3-D inserts

To achieve wedge-angled borders, all corners require eight wedges (two mirrored pairs short, two mirrored pairs long). The wedges either overlay the quilt or overlay borders of the quilt. The position of the overlay affects the illusion of the quilt's size. The wedges are inserted in border seams that may be appliquéd flat or left as dimensional flaps. At left, the wedges are positioned over the central quilt. At right, the wedges are positioned over borders with corner blocks. The border width, wedge size, and central quilt are equal in both quilts.

The wedges on the quilt overlay the quilt wedges basted to central quilt. Note the angled overhang of the raw edges on the back. Trim this overhang to match the quilt edge and add borders as usual.

Notice that the border width and the wedge size remain constant. This illusion of a central "ground" change reflects the wedge position as either an overlay or borders.

Wedge borders as background extenders require attention to grain lines. The outer edge of each expander wedge must be on the straight grain. Four cuts of each a North and a South wedge are needed to ring the central quilt area. The length of the wedges takes several calculations. Note: Because of its permanent markings, this process is easier with the 9-degree ruler. Measure the mandala. How much wider must the central area be? Divide by 2. Take a straight ruler across the horizontal lines of the wedge ruler (from the South end). Find that half measurement across the wedge ruler. This becomes the new South end of the wedge ruler. Measure the distance from the quilt's midpoint to the corner. Add the extension width measurement plus 1 inch; this is how long the wedge extension must be from the new South end of the wedge ruler. This is half of (midpoint to corner) a side extension. Cut four North/South pairs with one side of the wedge on the straight grain. Stay stitch 1/4 inch from the wedges' bias edges. Press the 1/4 inch to the wrong side. Secure the background to the work surface with masking tape (see Mounting the Doughnut Background, page 77). Taping prevents the central area from shifting while pinning the wedge

extensions. Lap the New South ends of a North/South pair. It will be a dart-like 1/4-inch seam. This seam aligns with the midpoint of each of the quilts sides. It also aligns with a normal 1/4-inch seam line on the quilt's edge. Bias edges of the wedge pair overlay the quilt background. Straight grain edges of the wedge pair extend beyond the quilt and are parallel to the original edge the quilt. Check the parallel edge with a straight ruler. Be sure the extension measurement remains constant and does not dip in at the lap line. Pin the bias overlay to the quilt. Repeat for each side. Miter corners, gently release tape, and appliqué in place. Additional borders can be added if desired.

Wedge-angled borders can be appliquéd overlays of existent background areas. These overlays are decorative and not meant to expand the background. As decoration, the bias and grain lines pose no risk of stretching or distorting the quilt's outer edge. Raw edges of the wedge overlays are rolled to the wrong side, pinned, and then appliquéd to the background. After the next round of straight borders is attached, the background fabric is removed (see To Trim or Not to Trim, page 82).

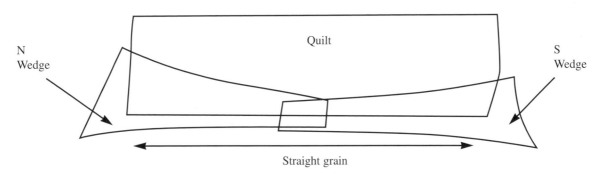

Wedges extend beyond the quilt edge. The amount of overhang equals the amount the background is enlarged.

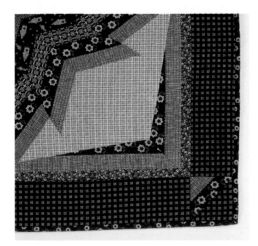

Left: Double Dish's wedge-angled borders.

Right: Pink Ribbons and Roses' wedge extensions.

Double Dish. Approx. 54" x 54". Pink/aqua/yellow on pink check. Combination cuts (45-degree, 60-degree, and Spokes) in Dresden measured lengths. This quilt has wedge-angled borders, tip additions on its spokes, and an eight-patch center. Designed and pieced by Sheila Finklestein. Quilted by Debby Lee.

WEDGE-CURVED CORNERS

Wedge-curved corners are an interesting border variation. Straight borders are added to the quilt, but curves are cut to replace the miter or squared corners. Each corner curve is constructed with ten (or six) wedge cuts and equals a quarter of a circle (see Rings and Frames, page 100). The doughnut hole used for curved corners can be any size. The larger the doughnut hole, the more open the curve on both the inside and outer edge. A 3-inch doughnut hole curve is the tightest curve possible with 9-degree (a 2-inch doughnut hole with a 15-degree wedge) and that which most closely resembles a regular squared corner. A larger curve (doughnut hole) intersects the sides closer to the quilt's midpoint. On a larger curve some of the design closest to a normal 90-degree corner will be lost.

Wedge-curved corners are cut from the same width strips as the straight borders they connect to. The edge of the border strip that connects to the quilt's center will be the inside curve, the doughnut hole edge. That inside edge will be pressed a 1/4 inch to the wrong side. After pressing the border strip, wedges will be cut from it using the 9- (or 15-) degree wedge ruler. Line up the pressed fold line with the doughnut hole line on the ruler (i.e., fold line on the South edge of the ruler). Cut ten (or six) wedges for each 90-degree angled corner. Each cut is made with the fold line on the same reference point/line. Only North cuts will be used. Each cut is seamed with the folded South edge tucked to the back. Thus the South edge will be seamed and clean finished while the North edge will still be raw. Curved corners overlay the central quilt then lap the straight border strips. Some of the quilt's corner area is eliminated; the fifth (or third) seam of each curved corner will fall on the bias/miter (diagonal of each corner) line.

The batting and back of a quilt with curved corners should remain straight grain and untrimmed to prevent stretch and distortion until after the binding is stitched in place. Borders with wedge-curved corners must be finished with bias cut binding. Straight-cut binding will not bend evenly around corners.

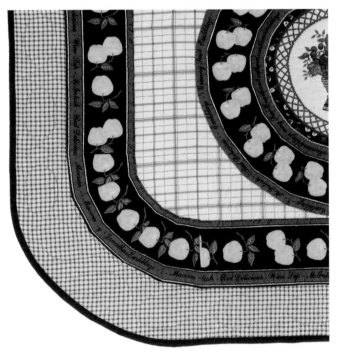

One of Country Platter's wedge-rounded corners.

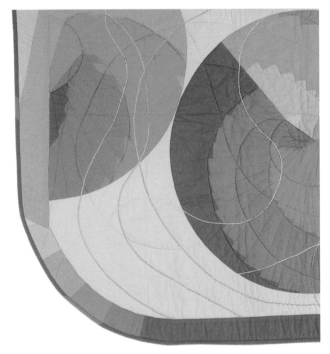

Rollout's wedge-rounded corner.

BASSACKWARDS BINDING

Bassackwards binding is a machine binding technique developed after much frustration with hand binding methods. Hand binding is time-intensive—it slowed down my completion time. It seemed contradictory to hand-bind an otherwise machine-pieced and -quilted project. It seemed much more consistent to stay within a machine technique. Traditionally, quilters have often chosen to apply the binding, either bias or straight grain, to the quilt's edge with a machine's straight stitch. Then the binding is rolled and "hand picked" to the seam line on the quilt back. It occurred to me that the "hand picked" technique was essentially the same stitch as that used in hand hems. I had, years ago, learned from Harriet Hargrave how to substitute a machine blind hem stitch for hand appliqué. This was the same process used on an edge. It took some experimenting and a "happy accident" to find a way to get machine binding to mimic hand binding. I had attached an entire binding to the back of the quilt instead of its front! When I discovered my mistake, there were no options left but to finish the quilt as it was—backwards. To my surprise, it was much easier to place the machine blind stitch invisibly in the ditch. It was easier to catch a tiny pick of the binding's crease.

❶ Cut binding (cross-cut or bias) double the desired width (this varies from quilter to quilter). Generally the cut width is between 2 inches and 3-1/4 inches.

❷ Seam all binding strips to each other with bias seams to reduce bulk.

❸ Matching cut edges, crease with an iron along the entire length of the binding strip.

❹ Edge stitch or triple zigzag all layers of the quilt together. Trim close to the stitching.

❺ Begin at the center of a side. Fold in 3/4 to 1 inch of the binding into itself.

❻ Apply binding with a machine straight stitch to the back edge of the quilt. Begin stitching into the binding strip, allowing the flap to hang free for now.

❼ Miter corners as you go.

❽ Insert the tail of the binding into flap, stitching though all thicknesses.

❾ Roll the creased edge to the quilt's front, slightly beyond the straight line of stitching that attached the binding to the quilt. Match the binding crease with that seam line. Pin closely every 3/4 inches.

❿ Blind stitch with nylon monofilament thread with the straight stitches in the ditch with tiny horizontal pick stitch biting into the binding seam and the binding. Manually stall the stitching progress at all miters to double-stitch the thick corners. Back stitch at the tail and flap joint.

⓫ Remove pins. Hand-whip the miters and joints closed.

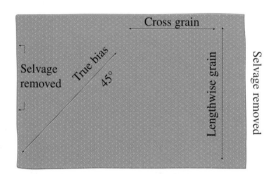

This shows the grain lines of the woven fabric and the ripped selvages.

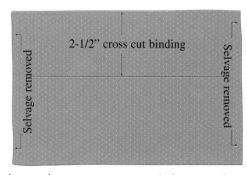

Shown here is the common cross cut (selvage to selvage) binding. The most common widths of the binding strip are 2, 2-1/4, or 2-1/2 inches.

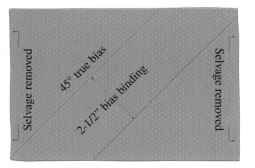

The bias cut binding width of the binding strip will vary, but 2, 2-1/4, and 2-1/2 inches are the most common.

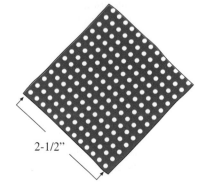

Binding strips are sewn end to end into one long unit. The bias seam reduces bulk. To position for seaming, lap at a right angle and sew diagonally across the corner.

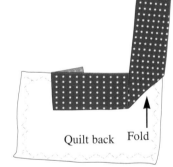

Trim the seam ("ear") allowance and press out flat.

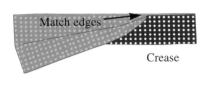

Fold along the length, matching ends.

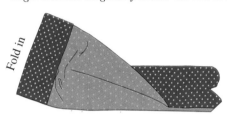

Fold in 3/4 to 1 inch at the beginning of the binding strip.

Whip along all edges to provide a solid edge to bind.

Begin binding at the center of any side, on the back. Start stitching 1 inch after the start of the binding. Stitch a 1/4-inch seam to 1/4 inch before the corner.

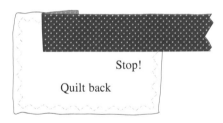

Machine-mitered binding. Stop 1/4 inch before the corner and remove from the machine.

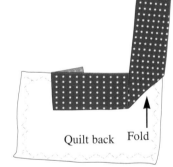

Fold, straight up, pulling slightly against 1/4-inch stop.

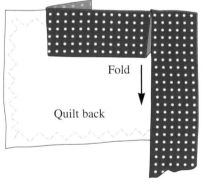

Fold down with the fold line, even with the raw edge of the sewn binding. Sew a 1/4-inch seam through all thicknesses. Continue to the next corner and repeat.

Tuck the tail into the open fold where the binding began

Roll to the quilt's front. Pin closely, matching fold to seam. Stitch with a machine blind stitch (hem the stitch in the ditch formed at the fold line). Stitch over all of the layers.

Curved corners must use bias cut binding. Overcast or triple zigzag the quilt edges to make a firm, stable edge. Fold back 1 inch at the beginning of the binding. Position the "foldback" on any straight side. Put binding on back (do not stretch) and stitch 1/4-inch seams.

Roll the binding to the front, match the fold line to the seamline, pin closely, and blind stitch in the ditch.

Tribal Shield. Approx. 45" x 60". Magenta/orange/black on burgundy. Spokes layout in measured (oval) lengths. Designed, pieced, and quilted by Sheila Finklestein.

Chapter 6

MORE MANDALA TECHNIQUES

This chapter is a starting point for the second- or third-time mandala maker. It assumes the mandala maker has had experience with identifying strata, is familiar with design terms and design layouts, and is adept at manipulating a wedge ruler. It covers techniques that refine your mandala as well as expand the design options available to you. This section also explores use of circle grid paper as a drafting and design tool. Circle grid paper is available in both 9- and 15-degree wedge layouts. Mandalas in this section use measured cuts, pivot points, and nonstandard curved tips to connect ragged edges. This section begins with clothing, special angles, and measured cuts and moves on to the more exotic oval and Dresden mandalas.

Creating Clothing with Wedge Rulers

Other options for wedge shapes and circle medallions also exist—as embellishment for clothing. Wedges pieced as sinuous trails add sweeping curves and are especially effective focal points. The wedge curves can be bold and dramatic or muted and subtle. These curves can be added to any portion of a garment. Wedge-shaped curves or circles can be either pieced into a garment's seams or applied to its surface with appliqué or trim. Wedge edges can be shaped or their lengths tapered to fit or highlight any placement on a garment.

To determine wedge or curve placements, it is easiest to work with full-size garment patterns and wedge pieces. Several options exist for accurate placement: 1) Working with a tissue paper dressmaker's pattern straight pinned together at the seams; 2) Working with a muslin fabric copy of the dressmaker's pattern basted together at the along the seams; and 3) Working with a finished garment.

Of these options, the muslin method offers the most accurate size and placement. Garment size and fitting alterations are done in this pattern stage. A muslin pattern allows easy visual check of the proportion and position of the curves and wedge shapes. Curved units can be equally divided between the top and bottom of the garment or clustered asymmetrically in one area. The curved design might parallel closures, follow hem lines, or mimic a collar. The added layers of fabric bulk in the curve units can be shaped to hug body curves. Curves can be shifted, ended, or begun in seam lines without damaging a paper pattern or the ripping and reassembly of an already completed garment.

To embellish a garment with curves and circles, begin with a dressmaker's pattern in a size that closely corresponds to your measurements. Transfer any expected alterations in the body or arm length to the paper pattern. Increase the side seam allowances to 1 inch to allow for any unexpected alterations. Pin the paper pattern to the muslin and cut out the muslin pattern. Then mark all darts, tucks, or easing on the muslin pattern. Using

Front and back view of a jacket embellished with wedges.

contrasting thread and an extra long machine stitch length, sew the muslin pattern into a garment shape. The muslin garment should contain both sleeves and shoulder pads pinned in place if required. Try on the muslin. Closure lines should be matched and pinned closed. Check the overall fit and make any fitting alterations.

In a full-length mirror (or with the help of a friend), position quarter-round wedge units in a pleasing arrangement. It is generally best to avoid the bust and the thickest parts of the body. Units may overhang muslin seams at odd angles. Consider whether an even wedge design unit or the garment's fit will prevail at each garment seam line. Pin curved design units onto the muslin. Remember to allow room for unit seams. Check the front, back, and profiles of the garment. Try several curve designs. If possible, record those options with an instant camera photo for later reference. Consider whether more or less curve units will "improve" your design.

When you have decided on curve designs, remove the muslin garment. With a pencil or chalk, outline the curved units on the muslin pattern. Units that overlap muslin seam lines must be marked with the seam's position; that overlap will be included in the garment's seam line. Seam the design curves together. Number the design curves and their corresponding places on the muslin and remove the extra long machine basting stitches from the muslin pattern. Use the marked and corrected muslin pattern to cut the garment fabric. Transfer all design curve markings to the garment fabric and number the curve positions. Match design curves to their placement lines and attach curves with trim or appliqué. Now, construct the remainder of the garment as usual.

The author models a wool coat, embellished with wedges, designed and made by Cindy Scott. Scott describes the coat: "The base (solid black) portion of the coat was a wool melton that I felted slightly by washing and drying once. The wedges were simply cut, with the smallest wedge ruler, out of old black and white felted wool sweaters (that Sheila got at Goodwill and Salvation Army stores). I threw in a little red for fun and zigzagged the wedges together (butt-fit, not seamed), then stitched them down to the base fabric, which had been joined at the shoulder seam. I added some black trim to the edges of the 'snail trail' wedges to help give it a clean look. I did pre-plan the placement of the snail trail before deciding on the width of the wedge, and I think I did scale down the size after testing, because the wedge was too big for going over the shoulder."

SPECIAL ANGLES

Special angles can be a choice or a happy accident. The 9-degree wedge ruler has two angle options permanently printed on it. The 15-degree wedge has angle suggestions printed in its accompanying book. Some stripes contain a motif with an interesting design angle that differs from any standard angle. The wedge can be positioned at any angle that follows the motif or makes it possible to enclose the whole "dominant" motif within the cut.

Motif angles are easy in the first cut. Position the ruler within the desired motif and cut. It is the copy cuts or the mirror of copy cuts that become a challenge. Marking your ruler with tape or a laundry marker will help this time but may get in your way on later projects. Caution: A laundry marker is permanent, and attempting to erase it with paint thinner or polish remover will damage your wedge ruler.

To get identical, matched wedges on special cuts, create an "invisible wedge," a dressmaking method for matching plaids. Begin by cutting the first wedge. The strata should be layered, matching motif right sides together for Chevron or mirrored cuts, or all right sides up, depending on which design layout was chosen. Layering produces pairs of cuts.

Take the original wedge cut and slide it across the strata until it matches the dominant motif and stripes. The edges of that first cut will seem to melt or become "invisible" when all of the lines match perfectly. Lay the ruler over the "invisible" wedge. Did the fabric wedge remain straight or did it shift slightly? If yes, adjust the fabric wedge, then reposition the ruler over it. Cut the new cuts, being careful not to skim off any of the original cut.

Continue to slide the original wedge along the strata, matching and cutting until you have enough wedges for your design. Make piles of pairs as you are cutting, ready to send the South end through your machine first. Do not move or handle these cuts more than absolutely necessary, because their non-traditional bias edges stretch easily.

SPECIAL CUTS

After reviewing the layout charts and trying your hand at one of the basic mandalas (as found in Chapter 4, Design Diary), you will be ready to try some mandalas with measured cuts. Measured-cut mandalas expand your artistic options with the wedge rulers to include ovals, squared Dresdens, and rings and frames. These mandalas are preplanned, using circle grid paper to plot and count the position and length of each wedge cut. Careful cutting and labeling are a must for these designs.

MULTIPLES

Several designs in this book use more than 40 (or 24) wedges to complete their design. Multiples are most easily made with wedges cut in a Sunburst layout where no matching of stripes is needed. Other designs like the Friendship Knot and Interlocken use both the North and its reverse South cuts. These designs are cut with a pivot point—a point where the center of your chosen strata occurs exactly halfway along the wedge size in use (i.e., a 16-inch wedge size equals 13 inches of distance along the ruler, so the pivot occurs at 6-1/2 inches). Placed at the pivot point, a pivot stripe will occur at the halfway point of both the North and South cut wedges. Units of North cuts can be seamed to units of South cuts, and the stripe will appear continuous, with no visual breaks. Bullseye cuts, with a pivot stripe, create smooth, even curves.

A Sawtooth layout using North and South cuts is more challenging. In Sawtooth layouts the pivot stripe must align with the exact pivot dot located on the North/South vertical marking of the 9-degree wedge ruler. The angle can be either the 45 or 60 degrees, but the exact center of the stripe must still hit the ruler on the measurement dot in order for the pivot stripe to be consistent in both North and South cuts.

Rocky Road. Approx. 30" x 45". Variegated blues on blue speckle. Spokes layout. Multiple medallion in snail trail design unit. This quilt has wedge-angled borders and a commercial bias edge perimeter. Its "sister" quilt is Portal (see page 10). Designed, pieced, and quilted by Sheila Finklestein.

To achieve a pivot point, you must first choose a strata. In this example, the "lace" is used; using the lace stripe the pattern "mirrored" out from its center providing four strata repeats, which was the best use of yardage. The pivot point is the exact half length of the ruler used (not half the planned radius!) and it occurs on the center "N"/"S" marking bullets. The original striped fabric (four strata across its width) is shown here.

A 60-degree Sawtooth wedge. The pivot point occurred in the center of the "lace" stripe. This piece is the chosen strata, stripped out (cut and removed) from the yardage.

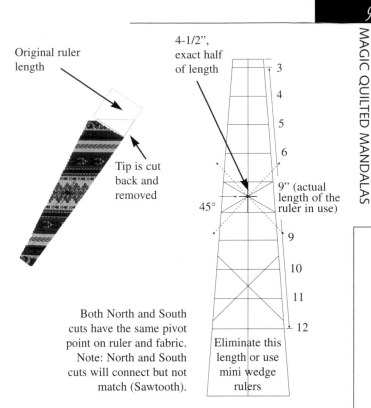

Original ruler length

Tip is cut back and removed

4-1/2", exact half of length

3
4
5
6

9" (actual length of the ruler in use)

45°

9
10
11
12

Eliminate this length or use mini wedge rulers

Both North and South cuts have the same pivot point on ruler and fabric. Note: North and South cuts will connect but not match (Sawtooth).

Interlocken. Approx. 15" x 22". Red/green/white with kelly green centers and spacers. Bullseye layout equivalent of multiple medallions. Its "sister" quilt is Santa Flag (see page 100). Designed, pieced, and quilted by Sheila Finklestein.

Graceful curves intertwine in Interlocken. It was constructed using the 9-degree wedge ruler.

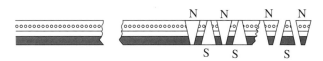

The 9-degree wedge ruler is placed squarely (Bullseye layout) over the strata. The wedges are cut with both the wide (North) end up and the narrow (South) end up. Individual wedge cuts are sewn into ten wedge quarter round units. These units consist of either all North or all South cuts.

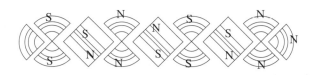

Quarter round units are crescent-shaped. These are combined with setting squares, the visual overlap areas of the design. The setting squares contain a length of strata plus enough contrasting fabric to make a square; the square is generally the radius measurement of the quarter rounds plus 3 inches. There are design holes at the base of the crescent-shaped quarter rounds. Plugs of contrasting fabrics are used to fill in these holes; they are usually the radius of the crescent's opening plus 1/2 inch (1/4-inch overlap plus 1/4 inch turn under).

The Friendship Knot is a variation of a classic fan pattern known as Mohawk Trail. Mohawk Trail uses quarter-round units to create its twisted path. I knew from the use of quarter-round shapes in the design that it should translate to 9-degree wedges, but I was not sure what would happen to the direction of slant when North units flipped into South units. Would the slant angle remain consistent, or would the angle's slant change direction? I was using the equivalent of three full rounds in this design. My yardage was limited by its availability. Trial cuts would eat up valuable inches. I turned to the circle grid paper to test my theory. First I sketched in the Sawtooth angle at the pivot measurement on a North circle and on a reverse designed South

circle. I labeled each quarter-round (N or S) and copied both circles several times. I trimmed each circle grid circle then quarter-cut them. I taped the seams, matching the broad North curve to the tight South curves. Does the angle of the stripes remain consistent or do those angles change directions somewhere in the design? If your pivot point is correct, the pivot stripe will appear consistent throughout and the North/South joints will be smooth with no jogs.

Notice the number of times that either North or South units are used in your design. Cut and construct the corresponding number of North and South units for your design.

Friendship Knot. Approx. 62" x 62". Blue/tan/black on cream. Sawtooth layout with Bullseye cut edge trim. Multiple medallion units (equivalent of three complete rounds). This quilt has vertical spokes at its star corners and corded Celtic quilting around friendship signatures. Its "sister" quilts are For My Friends and Friendship Flower (see pages 28 and 50, respectively). Designed, pieced, and quilted by Sheila Finklestein.

The following drawings show my design trial and error in circle grid paper.

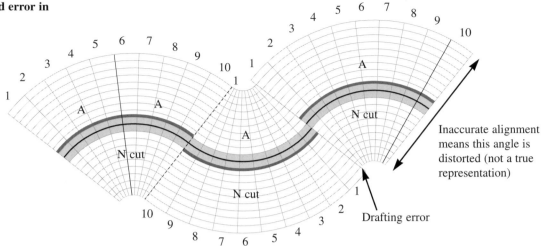

A Snail Trail layout is shown here using three ten-wedge quarter rounds. Count and mark the radius rings. Notice that the pivot stripe, while it does not align between the quarter of North cuts, it is not identical. Substitute South cuts in the center quarter round to make the strata consistent.

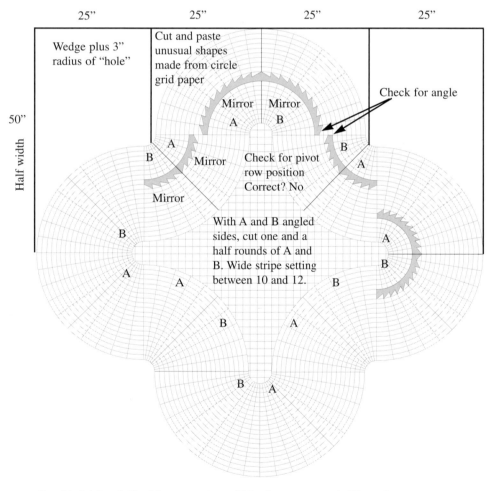

For this Mohawk Trail layout, mirrored North cuts are used. Here, the pivot stripe needs adjustment to be centered at "11" (pivot stripe on ruler length, not radius length). Notice that the Sawtooth will not remain on the outside unless South cuts are used. The accumulated distance and approximate size of this design is 100 inches square.

RINGS AND FRAMES

Rings and frames are an interesting variation of the circle medallion. Their wide-open central areas are perfect for interlacing or highlighting a print picture frame-style. Rings and frames are constructed from wedges cut from a very narrow strata or a single isolated stripe. Mandalas are usually constructed using the 6-inch doughnut hole as a important reference point, but rings and frames break that rule. The doughnut hole is stretched in rings or frames. The size of the central doughnut hole varies according to the space necessary to surround a print. With a ring you will usually know the space you wish to fill, the furthest distance, or outside dimension, that the design can fill without bumping into other design elements, or the borders.

A frame surrounds a picture or print; thus it is the inner distance, that of the doughnut hole itself, that is important. Measure across the midpoint of the print or block to be framed. Is that the longest distance? With a compass, take half of the longest distance and make a circle on newspaper or freezer paper. Positioning the sharp tip in the middle of your paper, stretch your compass so that the sharpened pencil tip is even with your halved measurement. Holding its tiny pin (handle) at the top, spin a circle onto the paper in the largest arcs (curves) possible without lifting the pencil from the paper's surface. Connect all of the arcs. Cut out the paper circle. Place the circle on a light box or tape to a well-illuminated window. Lay your print or cheater block over the circle. The paper circle will create a shadow behind an area of the print. Jockey that shadow until it covers the majority of the details you wish to remain visible. Is the shadow wide enough or too wide? Secure with a few pins and remove it from the light source. Trace around the final size "shadow." Remove the shadow and fold it in half, then in quarters. Measure the distance from its tip to the wide outer arc (curve) again. This is the distance to the finished inside edge of your frame. To add hem allowance the measurement will be 1/2 to 1 inch smaller (closer into the South hole). The actual thickness/width of the frame is the width of the strata. The distance across the picture and its frame will be the size of the "shadow" plus two times the width of the strata. If you have design size limits, check to see if that distance will fit. Can the strata be pared down, or must the doughnut hole be closed in? If the doughnut hole must be shrunk, what picture details will be lost? Resize your shadow to check.

To determine the size of the frame, measure the length and width of the center to be surrounded. Take half of the longest distance (4-1/8") and spin a compass circle on paper. Cut out the circle to make a shadow. Can the center be enlarged or cropped? In this instance (because the length and width are nearly equal), because the center is fairly uniform, a frame with the diameter of 8 can be used.

4-1/8" (half of the measurement)

(8.0)

8-inch frame in this case requires no additions
Length/Width (8.25)

Santa Flag. Approx. 22" x 30". Red/green/ white on white. Rings and frames layout. Large cheater panel center. Bullseye layout fan at base of design. Its "sister" quilt is Interlocken (see page 97). Also shown is the large cheater center panel. Designed, pieced, and quilted by Sheila Finklestein.

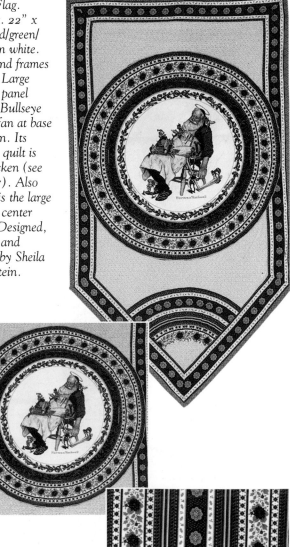

To make the frame, strip out your chosen stripe from the yardage.

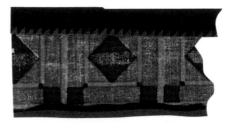

Roll and press a finished edge along the entire length of stripe (top and bottom).

Position ruler with its baseline marking along the lower folded edge of stripe and center the motifs.

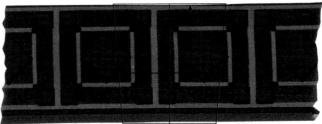

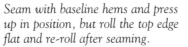

Cut all 40 wedges in exactly the same position and manner.

Seam with baseline hems and press up in position, but roll the top edge flat and re-roll after seaming.

Baseline

7

6

5

4

Note: This wedge has its baseline on 8. That means it is 8 inches to the center. Creating a ring with a 16-inch diameter doughnut hole.

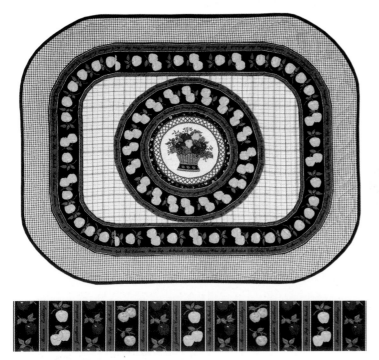

Country Platter. Approx. 30" x 45". Yellow/black/blue on gingham. Rings and frames layout. Wedge round corners. Also shown is the large cheater panel center. Designed, pieced, and quilted by Sheila Finklestein.

Decide which edge of your strata will be next to your picture. Fold under and press at least 1/4 inch on that edge, along the entire length of strata/stripe.

Find your "shadow" measurement on your wedge ruler. Mark that measurement on the ruler with sticky notes or tape. Place the ironed back edge of the strata/stripe even with the shadow measurement line. This line must be the same and consistent throughout the cutting (or the wedge cuts will vary in size!).

Cut from the folded edge straight over and off the strata. Cut 40 (or 24) wedges. Note: The sides of the wedge cuts will appear to be nearly straight—but they aren't. That tiny tilt will add up to a round.

Seam wedges into pairs, matching the folded edge. Do not press yet. Sew pairs into quarter-round units, then into a whole ring less one seam. With a dry iron, press open the seams. Be careful not to stretch the ring. Then press back a clean edge along the entire North edge (outer doughnut). On the floor or a large table surface, gently spread the ring. Do the edges of the final

seam match or must this seam be deeper? Slide the picture into place. Does the ring/frame conceal all raw edges? Make any adjustments in the final seam or, if the adjustment is large (more than 1/4 inch), distribute the adjustment into several (four or more) seams.

Tape the picture to a smooth surface large enough that the ring/frame will not drip over its edge. Position the ring/frame over the picture. Place the fat, final seam in the lower left hand side. This is a visual blind spot (where minor mistakes and variables are least likely to be noticed).

Weight the ring in place with several rotary rulers. Closely pin the ring/frame to the picture at the fold line. Machine blind stitch the fold line to the picture. The remaining edge will generally be machine blind stitched as well. It is recommended that the framed picture be applied to a single large background square similarly taped in place, but it is possible that the frame edge be bound or appliquéd to a pieced surface at this point as well.

Quilting Circles.
Approx. 90" x 90".
Black/green/purple on cream check. Rings and frames layout. The piecing was completed after the circles were inter-locked. Designed and pieced by Sheila Finklestein. Quilted by Sheila Finklestein and Piece in Time.

OVALS

Ovals are elongated circles. They are the natural fit for a narrow bed. They fill a rectangle without leaving awkward, empty background spaces above and below the medallion. Ovals can be made to any size by plotting them on circle grid paper. They can be short and plump or long with nearly straight sides, like a race track. Ovals are cut using measured cuts from the lengths determined by your circle grid sketch. Those measured cuts are sewn to their neighbors by matching the South tip of each cut. The North edges of each cut will be different sizes and will leave a ragged outer edge. That ragged edge will be skimmed off after quarters of the oval are assembled.

Ovals can be made with their cutting positions in any of the design layouts, and some are easier than others. Notice that after doing circle shapes that focus inward towards the center, the oval shape seems to shift the design focus to the outer edge rather than its center. It is important to have a strong emphasis on that edge, so that it does not appear to be a circle with tails on the top and bottom.

The Sunburst layout is a good design to emphasize the outer edge. Its striped design lines follow the length of the wedge ruler. The design appears to expand outward automatically with no matching of stripes. Matching stripes is more difficult in Bullseye or angled cuts, where the dominant stripe (the fattest or boldest) must be located on the perimeter of the oval. Because each wedge of a quarter round is a different measurement, the stripe will have a stepped appearance (like a drop match). The stripes nearest to the doughnut hole will develop an hourglass shape. This hourglass shape can be left as is or camouflaged with a large or especially bold center.

Neon Nightmare. Approx. 60" x 86". Neon pink/blue/orange on black. Sunburst layout with spokes in measured (oval) lengths. This quilt has a pieced border. Designed and pieced by Sheila Finklestein. Quilted by Piece in Time. Owned by Lea Thomann. An extra-long gridded oval was used for Neon Nightmare. Circles were pulled out from the center to estimate the size of the oval with the ruler extension. To achieve this, count the rings out from the center, cut to the maximum size for that position, and, when sewing, match the South ends; the North edge will be ragged.

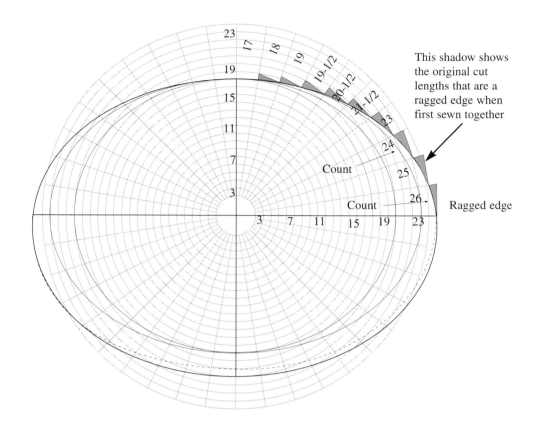

This shadow shows the original cut lengths that are a ragged edge when first sewn together

Count

Count

Ragged edge

To create an oval design with circle grid paper, determine the maximum length and width of the oval. With a design curve, sketch in the curve; on the curved edge you like best, count and number the grid rings out from the center. Create a "size needed" chart. Remember you will have mirrored curves and that wedges are cut to size and seamed together with a ragged outer edge.

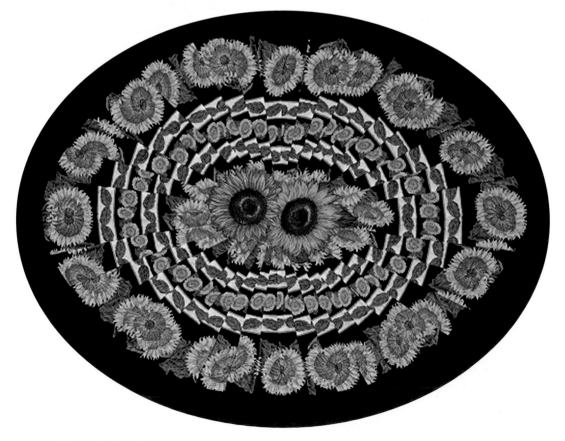

Notice the hourglass that develops in the stepped Bullseye cuts of Sunflower's center.

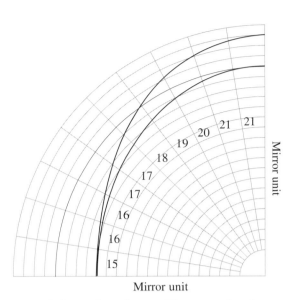

Mirror unit

Mirror unit

Ovals are easiest with the Sunburst layout. The outer edges "connect the dots" and can be single wedge spikes at the point tips or gentle single wedge scallops. Motifs worked from the outside edge in will leave a ragged "8" shape of the motifs near the doughnut hole.

Wedge size	1/4 x 4 =	Whole
15"	1	4
16"	2	8
17"	2	8
18"	1	4
19"	1	4
20"	1	4
21"	2	8

Need	Original size	+ added	Total
4	25"	12"	37"
4	25"	11-1/2"	36-1/2"
4	25"	11"	36"
4	25"	10"	35"
4	25"	9"	34"
4	25"	7"	32"
4	25"	5"	30"
4	25"	3"	28"
4	25"	1"	26"
4	25"	0"	25"

Ovals may be longer than the original 50-inch wedge length. To do this, add the length and width to smaller oval shape, increasing its dimensions in all directions or by adding only length and plotting (counting) the shape out on an extended circle grid. The count will be the most accurate nearest to the N/S vertical line. Extending the grid is done with three complete circle grids. Trim it loose from the background, mark the N/S vertical lines and slip the second and third grids outward along that line. Extend equally on both ends, then tape in position. Extend the wedge "seam" from the center grid onto the tails. Sketch in an oval shape and count and chart to reach the oval sketch.

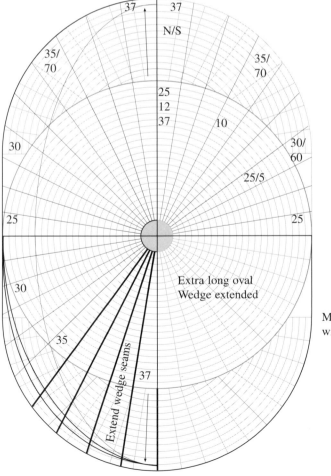

Maximum orignal
width 25"

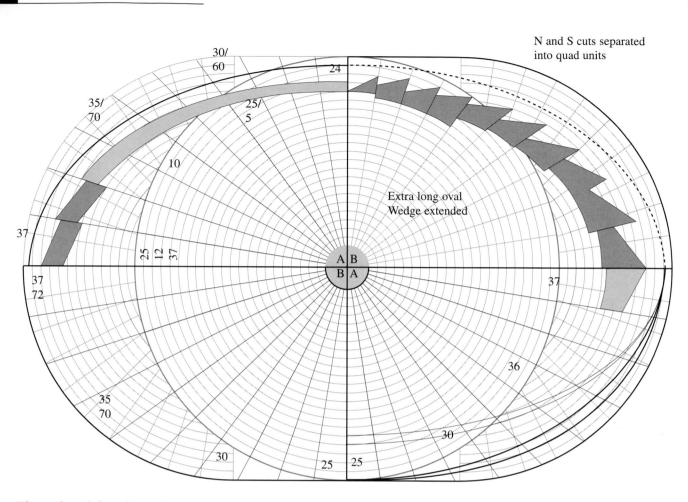

N and S cuts separated
into quad units

Extra long oval
Wedge extended

30/
60

35/
70

25/
5

24

10

37

25
12
37

37

37
72

35
70

37

36

30

30

25 25

A B
B A

This circle grid show designs in progress. Note the counted rings and the extended seam lines into the "tails." Also note the dominant stripe to give the ovals smooth lines and that **mirrored cuts are used for both straight and angled cuts in an oval**.

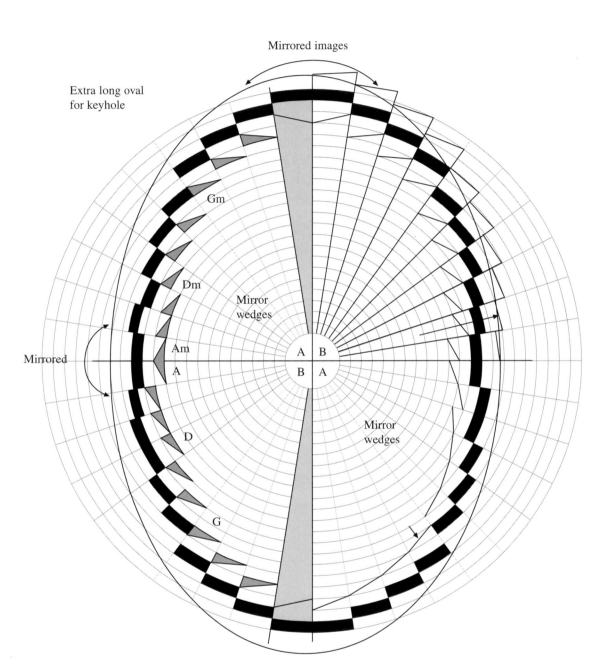

The Sawtooth layout in an oval is really cut as a Chevron.

Angled Sawtooth cuts are another possibility for an oval. Because a Sawtooth minces motifs beyond recognition, and seams intersect stripes at odd angles, the slip of the dominant stripe is less noticeable. Sawtooth ovals are cut in mirror image pairs. This allows the dominant stripe to remain at the same closed angle to the perimeter. Two pairs are cut for each position, then separated into right and left sides of the oval. It always helps me to lay out a half (with two of the same) on a large surface to verify their positions prior to sewing. Notice that right and left oval quarters alternate around the oval. As usual, wedges are sewn from the doughnut hole to the circumference, the ragged outer edge can be smoothed out or each wedge can be sewn into a spike (one wedge points) prior to sewing to its neighbors. Arrow tips (two wedge points) are not as effective as spikes for ovals, because the distance they leave between points seems too wide a gap for the eye to connect the dots.

To smooth the ragged perimeter, layer right and left quarter rounds. Match the peaks and valleys. With chalk or a pencil, connect the low spots along the perimeter. Trim with a scissors and correct any bumps or dents. Separate quarter rounds, then position and stitch into half rounds.

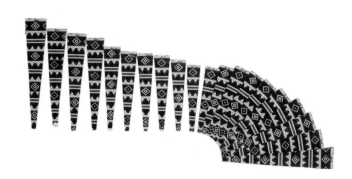

A straight-cut Bullseye for an oval equals a drop match. Note the design "chop" at the doughnut hole.

Open strata and motif tips do not reinforce the design perimeter. Compare the ends; notice how this Sawtooth cut leaves the tips open. (Note that the seams were not removed in this sample, causing distortion in the doughnut hole size.)

Sixty-degree mirrored cuts are measured cuts that match from the perimeter in. Note that the doughnut hole "chop" begins to form a figure-8. Also notice the closed tip where the angle of the motif/strata falls parallel to the cut tip.

Scarab, a quilt in progress, is lightly pinned to
its background. Also shown here is a close-up
of its single wedge tips.

WHAT IF I am making a fan and I do not want a seam down its vertical center?

Partial wedges can be added on both the East and West of the center vertical axis to fill out the number of wedges needed for a half round. A partial is several wedge-shaped sections sewn together to equal the size of the original wedge in use. The easiest partial is a wedge cut only half the width (plus seam allowance) of the wedge ruler or pattern in use. A partial can be treated as an independent narrow wedge or as a sewn addition to a regular wedge similar to the Floral Fan. A partial can be put in any spot, East or West, of the central axis, but there must be a corresponding split tip on both sides. This keeps the curve even and the design balanced.

A partial wedge can be added as a design element. As a design element, that partial wedge provides a cap or visual finish for a previously cut wedge. A partial is often a single stripe in a uniform width. It is usually narrower than a split tip and, added at the seam line, it increases the perimeter circumference of the medallion. This partial may somewhat distort a quarter- or half-round unit by causing overhang of the sewn unit beyond what is a normal 90 (1/4 round) or 180 (1/2 round) degree unit. Overhang can be corrected by increasing seam depth at the 1/4 and 1/2 round seams.

Floral Fan. Approx. 30" x 45". White/smoke blue/peach on coral. Bullseye layout with spokes. Spare parts filled out and completed insufficient yardage. This quilt has a four-patch center and scallop-shaped perimeter tips. Designed, pieced, and quilted by Sheila Finklestein.

*Twisted Ribbon Fan. 48" x 60".
Blue/red/green/cream on cream. This quilt uses a
combination of special angles and special cuts.
The angles in wedge cuts were tipped and moved
to make the stripes match. Its "sister" quilt is
Castle Keep (see page 12). Designed and pieced
by Sheila Finklestein. Quilted by Debby Lee.
Owned by Cindy Scott.*

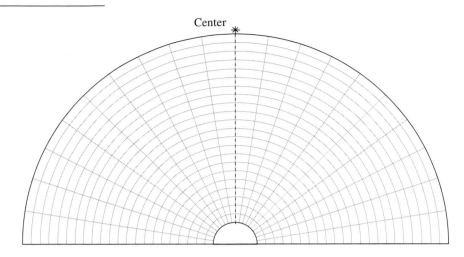

Normal fan-shaped layout. It has a central seam bisecting the design.

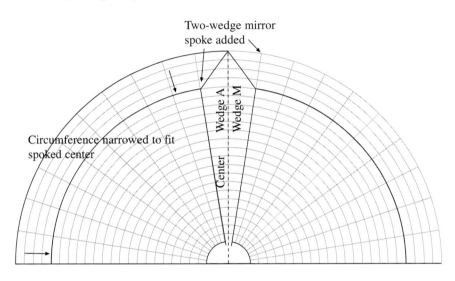

Normal 20-wedge fan-shaped layout. It has two wedge spokes added to the center.

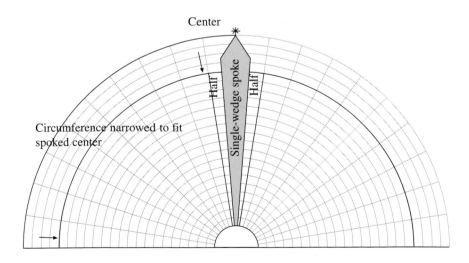

This fan has a centered spoke (19 wedges plus two half wedges). A double-wedge spoke is changed to a single centered spoke. It requires two half-wide spokes to balance and complete the half round.

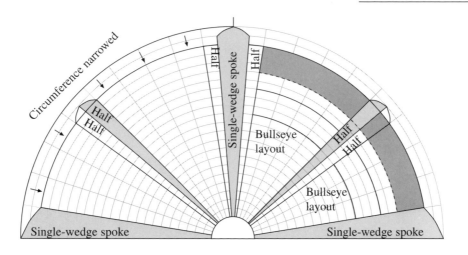

Fans. Additional spokes are added to the base and mid-fan (four half or "split" wedges, three single wedge spokes, and 14 single wedges).

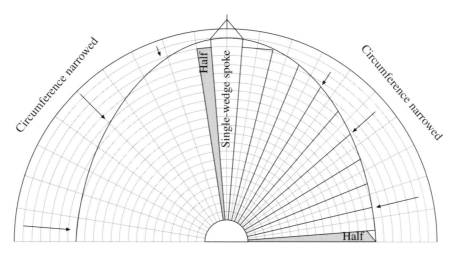

Fans may be elongated or oval variations. East/West sides will be mirrored cuts in either straight or angled cuts. Sketch in the desired oval and count and chart the needed sizes. Two split wedges can be added as an emphasis at the center or baseline for an oval fan.

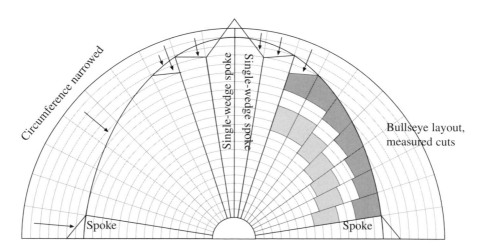

Oval fan. The dominant motif or stripe will be "stepped" and not continuous in both angled and straight cuts. An extra-wide stripe that appears at the perimeter will soften the "stepped" appearance that occurs due to measured cuts. Wedges cut with the Bullseye layout for an oval will have "stepped" appearance due to measured cuts.

MAGIC QUILTED MANDALAS

DRESDENS

Dresdens are another interesting shape that can be drafted with circle grid paper and cut in measured lengths with wedge rulers. Dresdens can be round, heart-shaped, or square. They can be drafted to fit any design limitations within the 70-inch diameter limit of the 9-degree wedge ruler and its extension or the 50-inch diameter of the 15-degree wedge ruler. Similar to an oval, the design emphasis of a Dresden is on its perimeter, but Dresdens also generally have a strong central axis. That axis is usually handled as spokes with arrow points that further highlight their position (see Tip Variations, page 58). The area between the spokes is made with measured wedges in lengths determined by the circle grid sketch. Those measured lengths are sewn from the doughnut hole out, leaving a ragged perimeter. The perimeter is generally trimmed down with a gentle curve connecting the low spots across several wedge cuts (see Crullers, page 62).

Dresdens work well in a Sunburst layout where the stripe runs the length of the wedge and motifs can be spaced to fall evenly with the perimeter. Sawtooth and Chevron layouts work especially well in Dresdens, their mirrored cuts reinforcing the design's perimeter emphasis. Careful consideration of the angle of stripe to the edge is important.

First decide what perimeter shape your Dresden will have. Next determine what size space the Dresden will fill. Usually there is a length and width limit of either a wall or bed surface. Plot that square or rectangle measurement over the center of the circle grid paper. Remember that the concentric rings occur at 1-inch intervals.

> 14" Spoke cut 8 wedges (or 4 + 4 mirrored)
>
> 10" Spoke cut 16 wedges (or 8 Spokes and 8 wedges)
>
> 11" Spoke cut 8 wedges
>
> 12" Spoke cut 8 wedges
>
> *The diameter of this Dresden is 28"

Pink Ribbons and Roses. Approx. 60" x 60". Pink/burgundy/blue on pink. Dresden layout with spokes ("resized"). This quilt has a four-patch center. Designed, pieced, and quilted by Sheila Finklestein.

When using a square Dresden, the length of the square's side is an important design limitation. That measurement either matches the square area the Dresden is to be mounted or, if the Dresden square is "on point," that measurement is multiplied by 1.41. The multiplied measurement is then plotted over the circle grid and the dots are connected into a square (the sides of the square should be close to the original side limit).

This chart shows the number of wedges cut in each measured position for both a quarter round section and multiplied by 4 for a full Dresden. The diameter of this squared Dresden is 50 inches.

THE 9-DEGREE DRESDEN

1/4 ROUND	FULL ROUND	
CUT SIZE	NUMBER OF WEDGES	
15 inches	4	16
17 inches	2	8
18 inches	2	8
25 inches	2	8

*The longest wedges are often cut as spokes in a Sunburst or Chevron layout.

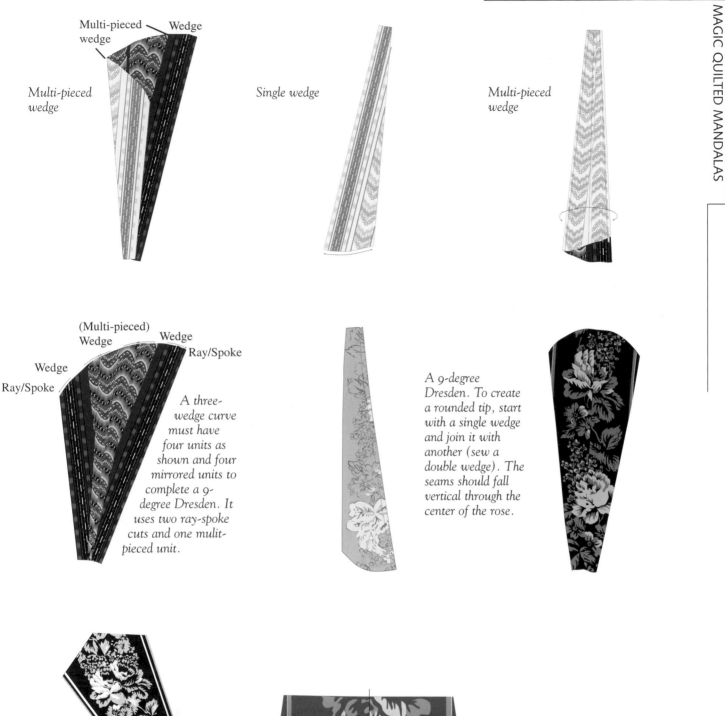

Multi-pieced
wedge

Multi-pieced
wedge ⸺ Wedge

Single wedge

Multi-pieced
wedge

(Multi-pieced)
Wedge ⸺ Wedge

Wedge
Ray/Spoke

Ray/Spoke

A three-
wedge curve
must have
four units as
shown and four
mirrored units to
complete a 9-
degree Dresden. It
uses two ray-spoke
cuts and one mulit-
pieced unit.

A 9-degree
Dresden. To create
a rounded tip, start
with a single wedge
and join it with
another (sew a
double wedge). The
seams should fall
vertical through the
center of the rose.

Two wedges; short Dresden spoke

The long point of the 9-degree Dresden.
The spoke or ray placement . Two wedges
are seamed, showing "new" roses
"rescaled" by the cutting of the wedges.
There is a pointed tip.

Curved tip of the Dresden plate.

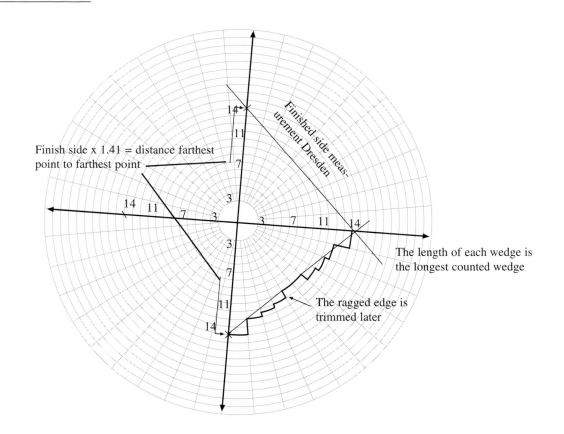

Finish side x 1.41 = distance farthest point to farthest point

Finished side measurement Dresden

The length of each wedge is the longest counted wedge

The ragged edge is trimmed later

To determine the Dresden's size, either plot an "X" over the circle graph and count the rings and connect the points, or begin with the finished side length (x 1.41 for plotting).

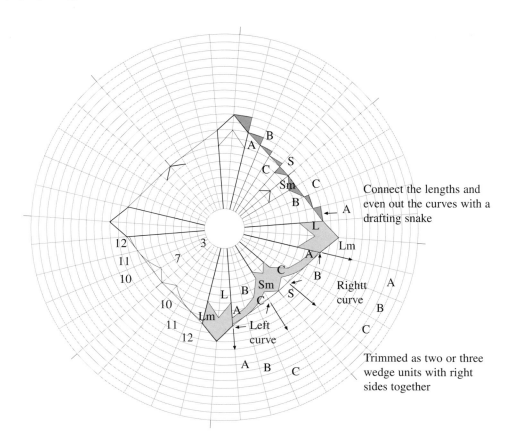

Connect the lengths and even out the curves with a drafting snake

Rightt curve

Left curve

Trimmed as two or three wedge units with right sides together

Dresden. Plot a square with eight long and eight short spokes. Sides may be cut as four mirrored pairs of each (A, B, and C). Note: A 12-inch grid equals a 24-inch diameter.

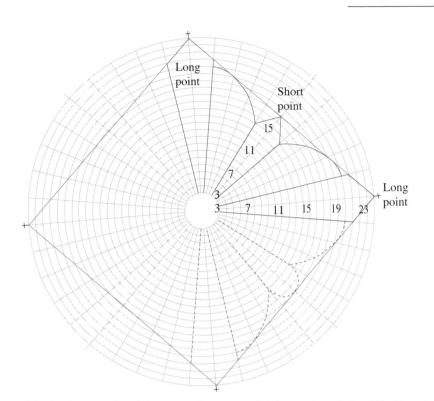

Dresden shape. Quarter then eighth the design grid and determine the size needed (original 25-inch grid). Drop in a square over the circle grid. Sketch in points at the long and short quarters. Connect the curves over the three middle wedges. Now count the grid rings from the center out to the desired size. Mark points and drop connecting lines between them, connecting the points. All eight wedges that form the long points are generally a pair sewn (mitered). The short points may be curved or mitered. Multi-wedge units are sewn to their neighbors, matching the South ends. The North ends will be ragged because they are cut to a variety of measurements. Press the multi-wedges well—use a template or curved ruler to make a curve connecting the long and short point unites; mark and hem. Layer the two units right sides together, hold firmly, and rotary cut through both mirrored units. Machine stay stitch on the hem line, press on the stay stitch to the wrong side, seam to long and short points, and adjust the hem's curve if needed to evenly connect the points.

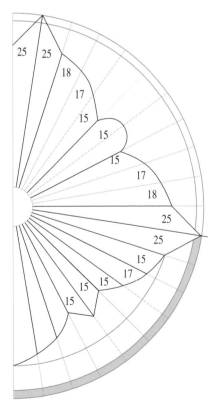

Counted grid rings provide an approximate length of wedges used.

Rose Rhapsody. Full-size bed quilt. Black/gray/beige mandala technique. Chevron layout. Pieced, appliquéd, and quilted by Kathleen Clark. Quilt belongs to Claudia Douds (daughter).

Chapter 7

CONCLUSION

The more I work with mandalas, the more I recognize circular patterns and designs swirling through my daily life. I recognize their calming, almost hypnotic, effect on people. I remember that cultures around the globe have instinctively chosen mandala symbols to represent a spiritual center in their lives. I remember the creation of any mandala is a growth experience and that each experience spirals us to a higher level of existence. I realize that these mandalas created with striped fabric and the 9- or 15-degree wedge ruler are just one of many techniques for making mandalas. I recognize thousands of possible variations within this single technique. I realized that there are as many variations as there are quilters and strata and that this single technique is easy enough for the beginner, yet intriguing enough for the long-time quilter. I hope you have found joy, in both the mandala process and its product. I hope you find that joy rippling over into all areas of your life, healing your creative spirit and becoming your own "medicine wheel"!

LOSSARY

Angled cuts: Wedges cut with the strata following either the 60- or 45-angled design lines of the ruler.

Angled sets: Cutting groups where the wedge ruler falls at either 60 or 45 degrees to the stripe. Sawtooth and Chevron (both with 45- and 60-degree variations) are examples of angled sets.

Auditioning: The positioning of fabric in an area to see if it "fits the part."

Bullseye: A straight-cut layout that forms concentric circles.

Chevron: An angled cut of mirrored pairs that forms arrow-shaped concentric circles.

Concave: Inside or "caved in" curves.

Convex: Corners or outside curves.

Cruller: Any variety of curved or scalloped North edges.

Cutbacks: The method of shortening a previously cut wedge.

Decagon: A ten-sided closed shape having ten equal angles connected by ten straight sides. Often used as fill for the doughnut hole.

Diameter: The distance across a circle from one side through the center to the other side.

Doughnut: A reference to the shape of a mandala without its center filled.

Doughnut hole: The open area in the center of a mandala; the empty central space not covered by wedge cuts.

Even stripe: A stripe that is matched evenly in both directions.

Exact trim: Trimmed edge that occurs at the time of cutting the wedges. It happens when the wedge ruler is completely within the strata and is trimmed around all four sides.

15 degrees: 1/24 of a circle (15 degrees x 24 = 360 degrees)

Hexagon: A six-sided closed shape, having six equal angles connected by six straight sides. Often used as fill for the doughnut hole.

Invisible wedge: The method for getting exact duplicates of a pattern or motif.

Mandala: A design radiating out from a definite center, usually a circle, but crosses, Dresdens, ovals, and stars are all variations. This term is used for both the center (medallion) of the quilt and the entire quilt.

Medallion: A dominant central design motif. It is often a circle, but crosses, Dresdens, ovals, and stars are also used.

9 degrees: 1/40th of a circle (9 degree x 40 = 360 degrees)

North edge: The widest edge of the wedge or its ruler. This edge is farthest from the center. It becomes the circumference or outer edge of the doughnut. The first wedge cut is done with the North edge up/at the top of the strata.

Octagon: An eight-sided closed shape, having eight equal angles connected by eight straight sides. Often used as fill for the doughnut hole.

Over shoots: The North end of the wedge ruler protrudes beyond the strata. The strata under the North edge of the ruler is not trimmed.

Pentagon: A five-sided closed shape, having five equal angles connected by five straight sides. Often used as fill for the doughnut hole.

Petal: A straight-cut, drop-match layout organized into set of cuts. Cuts may mirror or repeat in each group or petal. It looks like a flower.

Pinwheel: A straight-cut, drop-match layout organized into sets of cuts or blades. Looks like a child's toy.

Pivot point: Riveted to one spot, a place to change directions.

Radius: The distance from the center to the edge of a pie-shaped piece.

Sawtooth: An angled cut of face-up pairs. Ragged design looks like a saw blade.

South edge: The narrow edge of the wedge. This edge will be closest to the center, the doughnut hole. A reference point for trimming, it is the most accurate place to begin matching or machine stitching.

South cuts: Wedge cut with the South end of the ruler at the "top" of the strata.

Spikes or Arrows: Sharp angular points sewn at the North end of wedge cuts.

Spare parts: The waste at the beginning and end of each strata cut.

Split Tip: A straight-cut layout where an over-sized stripe bisects a wedge North/South.

Spokes: Visual punctuation used to break up the monotony of some designs.

Straight cuts: Wedges cut with the strata following either the vertical or horizontal design lines of the ruler.

Straight sets: Cutting groups where the wedge ruler cuts align to the stripe either vertically or horizontally. Bullseye, Drop-match, Sunburst, Swirl, Petal, Pinwheel, and Spokes are all examples of straight-cut sets.

Strata: Stripes. Narrow ribbons of color placed long-edge to long-edge (like stripes of the flag) are a strata. Usually strata is constructed by sewing together separate strips of fabric. Striped fabric is the fabric kit version of strata.

Sunburst: A straight-cut layout with the North/South center of the wedge ruler following the stripe.

Swirl: A straight-cut, drop-match layout where each of the 40 wedges has an individual drop.

Tips: The edge finish used on the North edge of the wedge cut. Tips can be a variety of shapes or finishes.

Uneven stripe: A directional stripe, with a "this end up" appearance.

Supplies and Quilting Services

DOHENY PUBLICATIONS, INC.
Marilyn Smith Doheny
P.O. Box 1175
Edmonds, WA 98020
(425) 774-3761
*9° Circle Wedge Ruler, extension, mini wedge set, and Circular Design Grid paper

MANDALI PUBLISHING
Monique Mandali
P.O. Box 21852
Billings, MT 59104
1-800-347-1223
*Mandala coloring books; original mandala line drawings suitable for quilting

PHILLIPS FIBER ART
Cheryl Phillips
P.O. Box 173
Fruita, CO 81521
1-800-982-8166
*Books using wedge tool techniques: *Quilts Without Corners*, *Wedge Works*, and *Compass Wedge*
*Wedge tools: 15-degree, 11.25 "compass wedge," and Circular Graph Paper

QUILTATIONS
Sheila Finklestein
211 Harcourt Dr.
Akron, OH 44313-6510
e-mail: Rfinkles@aol.com
*Lectures and workshops

QUINT MEASURING SYSTEMS
Carole Quint
P.O. Box 280
San Ramon, CA 94583
1-800-745-5045
*The Original True Angle Ruler, available in ten sizes

TWENTY-FIRST CENTURY QUILTING
Debby S. Lee
2727 East Shore Drive
Green Bay, WI 54302
e-mail: d2lee@aol.com
*Expert machine quilting of mandala designs on a GAMMIL industrial machine or hand guided on a Bernina

RELATED BOOKS

CELTIC QUILT DESIGNS, ADAPTED BY PHILOMENA WIECHEC
1980, Celtic Design Co.
834 West Remington Dr.
Sunnyvale, CA 94087

CREATIVE QUILTMAKING IN THE MANDALA TRADITION, DESIGN AND PATTERN DEVELOPMENT, JEAN EITEL
1985, Chilton Book Co.
Radnor, PA 19089

DRAWING THE LIGHT FROM WITHIN, KEYS TO AWAKEN YOUR CREATIVE POWER, JUDITH CORNELL, PhD
1990, 1997, First Quest Edition
Theosophical Publishing House
P.O. Box 270
Wheaton, IL 60189-0270

EARLY MEDIEVAL DESIGNS FROM BRITAIN FOR ARTISTS AND CRAFTPEOPLE, EVA WILSON
1983, Dover Publications
31 East 2nd Street
Mineola, NY 11501

EVERYONE'S MANDALA COLORING BOOK, VOL. I, II, AND III, MONIQUE MANDALI
1978/1991, Mandali Publishing
P.O. Box 21852
Billings, MT 59104
(800) 347-1223

HEX SIGNS AND THEIR MEANINGS, WALT
MAUER
1996, Garden Spot Gifts
302 York Street
Gettysburg, PA 17325

ISLAMIC DESIGNS FOR ARTISTS AND
CRAFTPEOPLE, EVA WILSON
1988, Dover Publications
31 East 2nd Street
Mineola, NY 11501

JAPANESE DESIGN MOTIFS, ILLUSTRATIONS
OF JAPANESE CRESTS, COMPILED THE
MATSUYA PIECE GOODS STORE
1972 Dover Publications
31 East 2nd Street
Mineola, NY 11501

JAPANESE EMBLEMS AND DESIGNS, EDITED
BY WALTER AMSTUTZ
1970/1994, Dover Publications,
31 East 2nd Street
Mineola, NY 11501

LOVE, MEDICINE, AND MIRACLES AND PEACE,
LOVE, AND HEALING BY BERNIE S. SIEGEL,
M.D.
1986 and 1989, Harper and Row Publishers
10 East 53rd Street
New York, NY 10022

MANDALA, THE ARCHITECTURE OF
ENLIGHTENMENT, DENISE PATRY LEIDY
AND ROBERT A. F. THURMAN
1997, Asia Society Galleries and Tibet House-
Shambala Publications, Inc.
300 Massachusetts Avenue
Boston, MA 02115

MANDALA FOR CONTEMPORARY QUILT
DESIGNS AND OTHER MEDIUMS, KATIE
PASQUINI
1983, C&T Publishing
P.O. Box 1456
Lafayette, CA 94549

MANDALA GARDENS, TEXT BY TARTHANG
TULKU
Amber Lotus Books
1241 21st Street
Oakland, CA 94607
(800) 3 AMBERL

MANDALA LUMINOUS SYMBOLS FOR
HEALING, JUDITH CORNELL, PhD
1994, First Quest Edition, Theosophical
Publishing House
P.O. Box 270
Wheaton, IL 60189-0270
*the bibliography in this one is amazing!

THE MANDALA SACRED CIRCLE IN TIBETAN
BUDDHISM, MARTIN BRAUEN
1992, Dumont Buchverlag GmbH and Co.-
Shambhala Publications, Inc.
Horticulture Hall
300 Massachusetts Avenue
Boston, MA 02115
www.shambhala.com

MARINER'S COMPASS, AN AMERICAN
QUILT CLASSIC, JUDY MATHIESON
1987, C&T Publishing
P.O. Box 1456
Lafayette, CA 94549

MYSTERY OF MANDALAS
1988, Heita Copony; 1989, Aquamarin Verlag
Theosophical Publishing House
306 West Geneva Road
Wheaton, IL 60187
(312)668-1571

159 CELTIC DESIGNS, AMY LUSEBRINK
1988, Scotpress; 1993, Dover Publications,
Inc.
31 East 2nd Street
Mineola, NY 11501

QUILTS WITHOUT CORNERS, CHERYL PHILLIPS
1992, E&P Sewing
135 N. Main Street
Gunnison, CO 81230
(800) 736-4281

ROUND ABOUT QUILTS, J. MICHELLE WATTS
1994, That Patchwork Place, Inc.
P.O. Box 118
Bothell, WA 98041-0118

SENSATIONAL STARS, GAIL GARBER
1995, Animas Quilts Publishing
600 Main Avenue
Durango, CO 81301
(970) 247-2582

SLICE UP A CIRCLE: EASY GEOMETRICKS FOR PATCHWORKERS, ANGELA MADDEN
1996, M.C.Q. Publications
19 Barlings Rd.
Harpeden. Herts. AL5AL. England
Quilter's Resource Inc.
P.O. Box 148850
Chicago, IL 60614
(312)278-5795

STRIPES IN QUILTS, MARY MASHUTA
1996, C&T Publishing
P.O. Box 1456
Lafayette, CA 94549

3 DIMENSIONAL DESIGN, KATIE PASQUINI
1988, C&T Publishing
P.O. Box 1456
Lafayette, CA 94549

WEDGE WORKS, CHERYL PHILLIPS WITH LINDA PYSTO
1997, Phillips Fiber Art
P.O. Box 173
Fruita, CO 81521
(800)982-8166

*I*NDEX